Change Without Pain

Change Without Pain

Pain

How Managers
Can Overcome
Initiative
Overload,
Organizational
Chaos, and
Employee Burnout

Eric Abrahamson

Harvard Business School Press
Boston, Massachusetts

Printed in the United States of America
08 07 06 05 04   5 4 3 2 1

Library of Congress Cataloging-in-Publication Data

Abrahamson, Eric.
    Change without pain: how managers can overcome initiative overload,
organizational chaos, and employee burnout / Eric Abrahamson.
        p. cm.
    Includes bibliographical references and index.
    ISBN 1-57851-827-X (alk. paper)
    1. Organizational change. 2. Organizational effectiveness. I. Title.
HD58.8.A265 2004
658.4'06—dc21

                                                    2003013430

The paper used in this publication meets the requirements of the American
National Standard for Permanence of Paper for Publications and Documents
in Libraries and Archives Z39.48-1992.

I dedicate this book to the executives of Deloitte Touche Tohmatsu, GKN plc, and the Sony Corporation, who have shown me by their words and deeds a new and less painful path to leading and managing organizational change.

Contents

Acknowledgments

A book recombines many people's experiences, assistance, ideas, and commitment.

In the realm of experience, there are the many, many leaders and executives with whom I have worked over the years. Even if I cannot acknowledge each and every one of them personally because they are so numerous, I owe them a profound debt of gratitude.

In terms of assistance, Columbia Business School and its dean, Meyer Feldberg, granted me the time and the support that I needed to give my full, undivided attention to this book. My editor, Melinda Merino of Harvard Business School Press, patiently, tirelessly, and diplomatically helped me bring this book to completion. Lucy McCauley was also invaluable in helping me with the mechanics of writing and editing. My agent, James Levine of Levine-Greenberg Communication, steered me deftly through the book publishing world.

In the realm of ideas, I owe a lot to countless people. Many are scholars in my field of organization and management theory; others are not. It is not the style, in such a book, to reference each and every one of them. I have, however, provided a bibliography of their work at ChangeWithoutPain.com.

In terms of commitment, there are the people who have always encouraged me to pursue my ideas when they were not fully articulated.

They are William Starbuck of New York University, Donald Hambrick of Penn State University, and Michael Tushman of Harvard Business School. Suzy Wetlaufer also recognized the potential in my ideas about change and, with the assistance of Diane Coutu, helped me publish an article on these ideas in the *Harvard Business Review*.

Finally, there are people who provided the book's inspiration: my father, Rodney Abrahamson, who by his example taught me to recombine any and all things into beautiful works of art; my wife, Valerie Campbell, and my children, Alex and Claire Abrahamson.

Introduction

Education is not the filling of a pail, but the lighting of a fire, according to Yeats; it is a learning process that involves pulling out knowledge, not putting it in.[1] This is particularly true when it comes to learning by managers and senior executives with years if not decades of work experience. I have had the privilege to watch CEOs, instructors, and other thought leaders ignite profound learning in such seasoned audiences. They did not destroy old knowledge in their audiences' heads in order to put in newly created knowledge. Rather, they helped them pull out what they already knew—their recent experiences and experiments, their newfound tricks and techniques, their successes, and their failures. They lit a fire that rekindled these audiences' interest in reconsidering existing knowledge, in recombining it in new ways, and in seeing it in an incandescent new light. This new light illuminated courses of action that their audiences had started to experiment with and which they knew, in their gut, led to superior outcomes—even if they could not fully articulate why. Over the years, these star leaders and professors had become masters of their trade because they learned as much from their audiences as they helped their audiences learn from themselves.

Superior instruction brings about successful personal change. This book examines how to bring about successful organizational change. In it, I share what executive audiences have taught me about the change management process over the last twenty years. I have been lucky to learn from the executives and employees of three companies in particular—one European, one American, and one Asian—to whom this book is dedicated. They are GKN plc, the large, United Kingdom–based automotive and aerospace engineering firm; Deloitte Touche Tohmatsu (DTT), one of the big U.S. accounting firms; and the Sony Corporation of Japan. I have taught and consulted for many other companies over the last two decades and learned similar lessons. But these three companies, more than all others, have shown me by their deeds that there exists a very different approach to managing change, an approach that stands in stark contrast to the current approach to change management portrayed in bevies of books, articles, and courses on the topic. This alternative approach has remained cloaked in darkness over the last few decades because the current approach to change management has grabbed the limelight for so long.

My fondest aspirations for this book are threefold. First, I hope that it can make a strong case for this alternative approach to change, which is based on the premise that organizational change, like education, can be a process of pulling out rather than putting in. This approach recognizes that organizations frequently have, in-house, all the existing people, processes, structures, cultures, and social networks they need to bring about change. It relies on discovering and pulling out these existing organizational assets, redeploying them, and recombining them to reach new ends. It is an approach that we easily overlook, but which we already know, in our gut, can produce superior results. I call this alternative approach to change *creative recombination* to distinguish it from the current approach to change, which a recent management book so aptly called change by *creative destruction:* change that destroys and removes existing organizational assets to make room for and fill these organizations with newly created ones.[2]

Second, I hope that I can convince you that destroying in order to create is not the only option, nor is it always the best one. I hope that as you finish this book, you will agree that the path to bringing about change, whether large, medium, or small, is not to destroy and replace by downsizing people, reengineering processes, revolutionizing structures, reacculturating entire workforces, or replacing social networks with computer networks. If anything, a growing body of careful empirical research, which I refer to throughout this book, supports our gut feeling that in many situations, such highly destructive, destabilizing, and painful changes can hurt more than they help. I hope that as you finish this book, you will prefer a second option: creative recombination, that is, pulling out what you already have and recombining it in a new and successful fashion. "Use it up, wear it out, make it do, or do without," as the old proverb goes.

In short, my first two aspirations are to remind executives that creative recombination can provide a less destructive, destabilizing, and painful path to bringing about change than creative destruction. My third aspiration is to challenge an old and worn cliché that too often dictates how we judge whether a leader, manager, or employee reached a goal using the best change process. This "no pain, no change" cliché is used to justify successful and unsuccessful changes alike when they are achieved at tremendous financial and human costs to organizations: "The change succeeded but the organization failed. Well, you know: No pain, no change." These kinds of change processes, even when they achieve their objectives, squander a firm's precious and limited resources, which are necessary to make more changes. These kinds of changes, therefore, harm not only routine operations to serve customers, but also the capability of firms to make more successful changes and to make recurrent change sustainable.

If DTT, GKN, and Sony executives taught me one lesson, it is that we must counterbalance the fatalism of "no pain, no change" with an ideal of "change without pain." This ideal should be the benchmark for judging how well a leader, manager, or employee managed a change. Change without pain is a benchmark that, even if it is unreachable, leaders and managers must aspire to today.

Why today? Because, to put it bluntly, in these days of perpetual gut-wrenching change, less pain enables more change. As I will show throughout this book, less pain enables the sustained *series* of successful changes that adapt firms to their ever-changing environments. I believe that the change without pain ideal is what sustains a DTT rather than creating an Andersen. It is what differentiates a Sony from a Time Warner. It is what makes GKN the second-oldest listed company on the U.K. stock market.

Before moving to the substance of the book, two important caveats are in order. First, I not only work with firms as a teacher and consultant, but also study them as a researcher. I also work in one: the Columbia

Business School of Columbia University, an institution with a mission not only to teach and cultivate existing knowledge but also to develop new, scientifically validated knowledge and insight. Over the last fifteen years, in my role as a scientist and researcher, I have carried out a series of carefully controlled scientific studies on the creation, popularization, and utilization of management techniques like the ones presented in this book.[3] I have studied, along with a growing number of other scientific researchers, how new management techniques gain and lose popularity.[4] Together, we have studied how consultants, professors, journalists, and executives-turned-authors discover these techniques. We have studied how books, articles, courses, and consulting engagements disseminate them. Finally, we have examined how leaders, managers, and employees use these techniques, and how long (or transitorily) techniques remain in use.[5] At this point, many of us want to put into practice what we have learned in order to share the techniques we have seen work in practice in a more lasting and effective fashion.[6]

Clearly, a large global industry provides advice to managers. The competition is fierce and cutthroat. To stand out in the crowded idea market, books and articles often overpromise. They present "new and improved" techniques as the only way to proceed and claim that these techniques are cure-alls: They do everything and work everywhere, with minimal effort and maximal results.[7] No technique, of course, can live up to this promise. After a few years and many unrealized expectations, commentators label the technique a management fad and even the very best techniques fall out of fashion, making room for another round of faddish overselling.

What does this research mean for this book? The answer seems simple: Don't write a book about creative recombination that oversells its potential and undersells creative destruction's potential. The truth, in fact, is much more complicated. Creative destruction has already been so oversold, so overgeneralized, so unquestioned and unchallenged that only a book that makes a no-holds-barred argument for creative recombination has the faintest chance of being heard. When "no pain, no change" has become a cliché, there is little choice but to start another cliché: "Change without pain." However, a book entitled *Change Without Pain* that is published by a reputable publisher must go well beyond countering old clichés with new clichés, fighting overselling by overselling, and debunking the creative destruction fad with the creative recombination fad. On the one hand, it must make the strongest case possible to present change by creative recombination as an alternative option. On the other hand, it has the responsibility to do so while reminding the reader repeatedly of one key point: The first option—creative destruction—is not so much *wrong* as it has been *overgeneralized* in countless books, courses, and articles.

Let's be very clear: Creative destruction may be necessary, and even preferable, in *certain* situations. In *certain* cases, it may even provide the best approach to the change without pain ideal. Creative destruction is not, however, the *only* option. Like creative recombination, leaders and managers must use it judiciously, at the right time, and in the right balance. In the final analysis, senior executives will have to strike this optimal balance between when and how much creative destruction and creative recombination they employ, given the idiosyncrasies of their situation and how much pain their firm can tolerate. It will be a hard and artful task, but, without being flippant, that is why executives make the big bucks.

A second caveat is in order. The discerning reader will have already noted the two obvious challenges that face a book, like this one, that advocates changing how we change. First, and rather amusingly, it has to counter those who would dictate change by creative destruction as the only option for change. In my experience, the creative destroyers can be quite resistant to revisiting and reconsidering cherished assumptions about change management—particularly when this requires the creative destruction of their own assumptions about change. Second, and more important, a book that advocates changing how we change must be self-consistent. It cannot warn against the dangers of creative destruction while leading a mad rush to creatively destroy everything we know about change management.

This book cannot, therefore, aim to creatively destroy creative destruction to make room for creative recombination. It must present an approach to changing change that both builds on and uses the very best change management thinking, tools, cases, and techniques that have preceded it. This book must reconfigure, recombine, and redeploy received wisdom about change management—in practice, in education, and in scientific research—in a way that is better fitted to our times.

Therefore, this book will reconsider, review, and recombine insights from the past, without wallowing in the past. It will revive cases that executives know well because they appear in many articles, readers, and seminars on change management—cases that, seen through the lens of creative recombination, can teach us new lessons about change management. Cases that urgently need to be revisited, reviewed, and reconsidered in a new light. Why urgently? Because organizational change has a massive effect on millions of organizations and puts the careers, livelihood, and well-being of billions of employees and executives at stake. What could be more important?

Change Without Pain

1 Organizational Change and Its Discontents

CONSIDER JOAN'S *career at Cisco Systems, the largest Internet backbone equipment provider in the world. I used to think that Joan's experience was an anomaly; I now find it so prevalent as to be satirized in every other Dilbert cartoon. Over the two years that Joan occupied the same position at Cisco headquarters, her immediate boss changed no fewer than eight times. Each of Joan's eight bosses came in with his or her own "new" change initiatives. Moreover, the vice president heading up her entire department changed three times, each VP launching a complete reorganization upon taking over. In the process, her department experimented with several rounds of prioritizing projects that went nowhere—among them, six sigma and e-learning, in which Joan was involved. With all these managerial changes, Joan stopped and restarted her e-learning project no fewer than seven times—about once a boss, that is. Ultimately, the project never saw the light of day, although Joan still believes Cisco desperately needs it today.*

What slowed the project? Not only the stopping and starting, but also the tendency among her revolving bosses to cut costs by outsourcing most programming and design, to then become dissatisfied with the results, and to then in-source, only to outsource again a few bosses later. In Joan's words, "The projects would switch from 90 percent in-sourced to 90 percent outsourced, and then three months later [switch] back again." In time, however, Joan realized that the change chaos slowing her down existed beyond her department and could be found in many parts of Cisco.

To his credit, Cisco's CEO, John Chambers, would deliver a clear compelling vision, with a clear and focused set of priorities, and would stick to them through thick and thin. However, as his message cascaded down the organizational hierarchy, each unit in this highly decentralized organization would add to Chambers's priorities its own "vital" initiatives. By the time Chambers's message reached Joan, the same question would face her every time: "Which of these twenty priorities do you want me to pay attention to, if I had a boss who would want to put a stake in the ground and empower me to make such a choice?"

What ultimately killed the project? Not just Joan's realization that endemic initiative overload would continue diverting her from completing her project. Much more important, Joan had realized that she had become a person she did not want to be: deeply cynical, burned out, political, and plagued by chronic work-related headaches. The project ended with the decision by Joan—a star Cisco employee with a Ph.D. from a leading U.S. university, a survivor who had outlasted no fewer than four rounds of Cisco layoffs, and an employee who remains deeply committed to Cisco and its CEO—to quit of her own volition.

Cisco is not an anomaly and it is perhaps unfair to single it out. It suffers from a rapidly growing malaise plaguing an increasing number of organizations today: what I call *repetitive-change syndrome*. The symptoms? Initiative overload, change-related chaos, and widespread employee anxiety, cynicism, and burnout. The results? Not only do relentless tidal shifts of change create pain at almost every level of the company and make organizational change harder to manage, more costly to implement, and more likely to fail, but they also impinge on routine operations and render firms inwardly focused on managing change rather than outwardly focused on the customers these changes should serve.

By *initiative overload,* I mean the tendency of organizations to launch more change initiatives than anyone could ever reasonably handle. When that happens, people in a firm such as Cisco begin to duck and take cover whenever they see a new wave of initiatives coming. Like Joan, they have learned the hard way that you can get labeled as "resistant to change" by arguing with a new boss that his or her pet project was already tried, tested, and found wanting only two bosses ago.

Change-related chaos, another effect of repetitive-change syndrome, refers to the continuous state of upheaval that results when so many waves of initiatives have washed through the organization that hardly anyone knows which change they're implementing or why. Moreover, because people change positions so frequently in these kinds of firms, the Joans of the world often become the only keepers of the organizational memory. They find themselves alone in pointing out one more pendulum swing between two alternatives, each of which has its costs and benefits—not only in-sourcing versus outsourcing, but also centralization versus decentralization, or product versus functional reorganizations, for instance.

Perhaps the most painful consequence of repetitive-change syndrome, however, is what it does to employees. Anxiety, cynicism, and burnout infuse the organization. This is no joke. To Joan's chronic headaches, add another close female colleague's hair loss, and a third's recurring ulcers.

In this environment, only senior managers and brand-new employees are enthusiastic about change. Joan and her ilk, who have seen one too many flavors of the month, one too many "new innovations" stop and start with little follow-through, become deeply frustrated by the continual disruptions in routine operations. As they take ever more time dealing with new initiatives, the day-to-day work of serving customers suffers. Meanwhile, the wake of continuous change pushes aside those organizational issues that need genuine attention. As a result, people like Joan become increasingly cold to any new initiative and end up creating their own inflexible organizational layer of human permafreeze: highly cynical and resistant to change.

Yet despite all of these ill effects, if you open almost any of the hundreds of books written over the last three decades on how to manage change in organizations, you will find "unrelenting change" as the common mantra, the very kind of who-moved-my-cheese change that abounds at Cisco. "Change or perish" is its rationale. An assumption underlies these messages: that people naturally resist change and that leaders should destroy or cast aside the old ways in order to create a spanking new future—a process aptly called "creative destruction" in a recent management book by that title.[1] Rarely do these books consider that unrelenting change and creative destruction might cause widespread disruption resulting in resistance to change by people like Joan. Rarely do they consider that what they call "resistance *to* change" is, in fact, "resistance *from* change." Indeed, with slogans like "no pain, no change," companies justify the continuous disruption that relentless and destructive change causes in daily organizational activities involving customers, suppliers, employees, managers, leaders, and other organizational stakeholders.

These advice givers (and the companies that follow them) ignore the scientific research coming out of business schools showing that many organizations change *and* perish.[2] Or, more accurately, they change and therefore perish. In certain cases, rapid and continuous change simply rips an organization apart.

Carefully controlled scientific studies indicate that the more frequently an organization changes, the greater its risk of failing.[3] Or put differently, the greater the interval between changes, the less likely that an organization will fail because of the changes. Moreover, in close to two-thirds of industries studied, rather than increasing corporate survival rates, large-scale creative destruction actually depressed them. Researchers have found that creative destruction hindered rather than helped the survival rate of newspapers, hospitals, airlines, wineries, savings and loans, automobile manufacturers, semiconductor manufacturers, bicycle manufacturers, Japanese banks, and even post-perestroika communist newspapers.

Am I saying that a firm such as Cisco should, now and ever after, halt all change programs, all efforts at improving its practices?

Absolutely not. Cisco lives in an extremely dynamic industry and needs to make repeated changes to adapt to the changing competitive environment. This book, therefore, starts from the premise that the continuous change, creative destruction, change-or-perish, and no-pain-no-change advice so prevalent over the last decades is not so much wrong as overgeneralized. It is still very useful, for instance, for the rare firm remaining in today's corporate world that has resisted change for too long and that may need to make many big changes quickly or face extinction. But it does not help firms like Cisco, which suffer from repetitive-change syndrome. To the contrary, it harms them and can even destroy them.

Indeed, for most organizations, change management advice has been too broad and unspecific to help much at all, leading companies to implement sweeping change initiatives with little concrete direction or hands-on tools. Most change management theorists have not provided help on how to lead and manage organizational change in a world of already excessive organizational change. Indeed, their change-or-perish advice only exacerbates the syndrome's harmful consequences.

This book attempts to remedy that situation. In it, you will find maps, tools, and techniques that will offer organizations a way to change without inflicting much change-related pain. More specifically, I intend this book for executives, leaders, managers, and students of management who want to avoid repetitive-change syndrome. It provides ways to change organizations—whether they are entire corporations, divisions, or departments—while minimizing not only change damage to their employees and the routine operations they carry out, but also change damage to these organizations' capacities to make still more nondamaging changes. In other words, the book provides a formula for sustainable change—repeated change that does not undermine the capacity to continue making repeated changes.

The book also targets executives, leaders, and managers who need not only to revive organizations suffering from repetitive-change syndrome but also to resuscitate employees like Joan, who have been put through the wringer of too many "new" initiatives and have been left with little patience and few inner resources to do their jobs well.

Before I suggest a new approach to change management, however, let's examine in more detail the origins of the current creative destruction approaches, the ways in which they remain relevant, and how students of change management must update them in order to manage needed change in a world of already excessive organizational change.

The Roots of Creative Destruction

Despite the appearance of novelty, most of the purportedly innovative change management prescriptions over the last several decades have simply been repetitions on the same theme. The fact is that change management advice has remained largely unaltered since the 1970s—a period when many U.S. firms, rendered dominant for too long by the military destruction of their prewar European and Asian competitors, needed leaders who could shake them quickly and aggressively from their complacency. Inwardly focused and excessively stable, these firms had become blind to the many changes they would have to undertake to survive the resurgent global competition of the 1980s and 1990s.

Consider the example of General Motors (GM) in the 1960s, a firm that had dominated car markets since the end of World War II. The key challenge for senior executives was not to beat external competitors—"Made in Japan" was a joke for them, and they could safely ignore non-U.S. competitors, or so they thought—rather, it was to defeat internal political competitors for promotion to GM's upper echelons. GM became the land of what it called the "nonobvious promotion." Rather than promoting executives who were most deserving, superiors gave the job to the most unexpected, and often least qualified, contender. These career-saving promotions indebted the nonobviously promoted to their superiors, turning them into their superiors' loyal political allies in future promotion and political contests. Insecure about how they reached executive rank, the nonobviously promoted would then demand a kind of obsequious obedience from subordinates.[4]

Lost in this inwardly focused, ritualistic, and pathological politicking was any inkling of the external threat from Japanese, Korean, and German automakers that firms such as GM and Chrysler would soon have to reckon with. Therefore, the change management practices of the 1970s had to focus on how to launch firms like GM onto the path to radical change. Such organizations had remained so stable, and so maladaptive, for so long that they literally had to change or perish. Indeed, in 1981, Chrysler posted the largest loss ever in U.S. corporate history.[5] Therefore, the advice was that organizational changes had to be big and destructive—what today we call *creative destruction*. To create a new hopeful future, such creative destruction had to cast aside all that was wrong about the past, whatever the pain. The pain was so intense, however, that the danger of backsliding into another period of maladaptive stability became a real possibility; thus, revolutionary change had to be followed by yet more rapid, continuous, destructive, and relentless changes in order to keep the firm more flexible and faster than its competition.

The result was a set of change management prescriptions that should sound familiar to everyone, since despite cosmetic alterations, they remain virtually unchanged today. The problem is that fewer and fewer such excessively stable firms still exist. Why? Because most leaders heeded the advice of relentless-change and creative destruction gurus throughout the 1980s and 1990s, creating firms that have been changing at full throttle ever since. Because of this pendulum swing away from the pole of excessive stability toward the relentless-change pole, a rapidly growing number of firms are suffering the consequences of repetitive-change syndrome.

One of the situations in which change-or-perish or creative destruction still remains useful is in firms I call *change avoiders*. Conversely, creative destruction can harm organizations, like Cisco, that have changed too much, which I call *changeaholics*.

Change Avoiders and Changeaholics

Organizations today that resemble GM in the 1960s have a dinosaur-like quality. They have consistently sought out only stability; as a result, they may indeed have to undergo rapid, relentless, destructive change by creative destruction or face extinction. One recent change avoider is the Koç Group, a Turkish conglomerate of businesses that range from automotive and related accessories to white goods and electronics, retail, finance, energy and mining, knowledge and information technology, utilities, and exports. As a senior Koç manager explained to me, Koç thrived until recently in protected markets— shielded from global competition and even from the pressure of the common market. It was helped by powerful ties to the Turkish government, docile suppliers, and the lack of serious European or global competitors in Turkey. As the Turkish economy continues to globalize, however, Koç faces an entirely new competitive environment, with new, powerful, and aggressive global entrants.

Firms like Koç must change urgently and most likely dramatically. These firms have to realize the trap they are in and walk through the valley of death. But change avoiders are becoming increasingly rare. Most have either become extinct or, like Koç, have realized the problem and are already well on the path to change—and, if anything, could well run the risk of excessive change.

At the other extreme are organizations like Cisco—the changeaholics with an apparently insatiable addiction to change. These changeaholics often suffer from acute repetitive-change syndrome. The resulting initiative overload, change-related chaos, and employee anxiety, cynicism, and burnout that build with each new wave of change render each of those change waves all the more disruptive, expensive to pull off, and likely to fail.

Consider the evidence. Cynicism has become so prevalent in organizations that it has spawned its own little field of academic research.[6] A host of other studies report widespread change-related problems, chaos, and initiative overload.[7] Likewise, there exists in excess of five thousand studies of employee overwork and burnout.[8]

The approach to change advanced in this book targets both changeaholics and firms at risk of changeaholism. My central argument is that reducing the amount of highly disruptive change will allow these firms to attain superior long-term and shorter-term performance. Such an approach will thereby enable more changes more easily, more cheaply, and with more success. It will, in effect, bring firms closer to the change without pain ideal.

How can organizations today, mired for so long in a world of already excessive organizational and environmental change, aspire to such an ideal? How can they hope to manage change periods in the least disruptive fashion possible? Paradoxically, by learning how to change how we change. More specifically, by learning two new techniques that create less disruptive and painful change.

One technique enables less disruption and pain in the midst of change. I call this alternative approach to change *creative recombination* to distinguish it from creative destruction, that is, change that destroys and removes existing organizational assets to make room for newly created ones. By contrast, creative recombination minimizes disruptive and painful destruction by using assets an organization already has and recombining them creatively in a new and successful fashion.

Creative recombination suggests an alternative, less disruptive, approach to change. I turn to it first and give it the lion's share of attention throughout this book. But there exists a second technique to reduce disruptive change and pain, a technique that reduces the *amount* of change. I call this second technique *pacing*—it alternates periods of stability and change, counterbalancing one with the other and delivering the benefits of both. Pacing, therefore, suggests when to change and when to stabilize the firm (industry conditions permitting). I turn to it in the latter part of the book.

Creative Recombination: A New Path to Change

Probably the best way to explain the concept of change by what I call creative recombination is to begin with a story that will provide the underlying metaphor for this book: the basement workshop. This story is about one particular workshop—my father's—and how my father fashioned a potter's wheel for me when I was a teenager.

At first glance, my father's workshop appears strange, maybe even messy. It is full of odd and mismatched parts: a scooter engine, steel bars, cogs, and old toys. You do not notice the hidden order to this apparent madness. In the workshop, each type of element can be easily located. In one corner, shelves overflow with carefully labeled receptacles containing all forms of washers, nuts, bolts, screws, nails, spikes, powders, oils, paints, greases, and solvents. In another corner, an antique metal forge uses a vacuum cleaner as bellows. It stands next to an anvil, a welding machine, and an inventory of scrap metal. Above hang three different bicycles over the skeleton of a scooter. In a third corner, there are piles of gravel, sand, and plaster of paris bags. A row of china inks of every possible color except purple are neatly lined up in the last corner. Next to them stands an architect's table that holds all forms of tracing tools. Above it, a bulletin board contains the pictures, diagrams, and related articles guiding a current project. The bookshelves contain volumes ranging from a treatise on the smelting of metals to Heidegger's *Being and Time* to a book on the optics of World War I bomb targets, all neatly arranged by topics.

When my father decided I should have a potter's wheel, rather than going out and buying me one, he went into his basement and looked around. In the part of the workshop that stores scrap metal parts, he picked up a metal disk, a rejected aircraft part he'd found in a flea market some years before. He also found a long, steel rod of automotive origin, which he welded onto the metal disk. He mounted the contraption on the frame of a washing machine whose engine, connected to the rod by one of my discarded leather belts, would spin the plate. Then, as I watched the washing machine engine come to life, my father threw a hunk of clay on the spinning plate and carefully molded it into a coffee cup. I was amazed—not so much by the fact that this contraption actually worked as well as the potter's wheel that I used in a professional studio near my home but by how quickly my father's careful organization of so many mismatched parts allowed him to locate the parts he needed and to recombine them in the midst of what looked, at first, like a chaotic assemblage of heteroclite stuff.

There was an iron-tight order and logic to my Dad's apparent madness—and therein lay the origins of my thinking about creative recombination and how I myself would be able to use these ideas, years later, in my own work about organizational change. The basement workshop is a helpful metaphor for change without pain because it highlights the key tools, skills, and techniques that enable an organization to achieve less disruptive change. How? By finding, reusing, redeploying, and recombining the mismatched parts that the organization already has lying around its corporate basement. Like any analogy, the basement workshop analogy contains parts that could convey the wrong impression. The impression I wish to create is not one of a chaos of rusty pipes and broken machines in which one cannot find anything except, on rare occasions, a few inferior solutions. The image, rather, is one of a well-run corporate basement, rich in high-quality recombinants that can be easily located, redeployed, and recombined to bring about smoother, more cost-efficient, and less painful organizational change.

Achieving change through creative recombination is not just a theory; the basement workshop is not just a hollow metaphor. My first lessons in creative recombination came from consulting and teaching with GKN plc, one of the oldest companies listed on the U.K. stock market. Over its history, the company has demonstrated an amazing capacity to recombine itself into new, highly successful configurations.

It went from smelting iron to making wood screws and metal screws. During the 1970s, it diversified in a number of unrelated industries. During the 1980s and 1990s it refocused on its core businesses. Its largest business currently is its Driveline division, the producer of constant velocity jointed (CVJ) half shafts for over 40 percent of the automobiles on the planet—the business that has been a key pillar of GKN's performance over the last thirty years.

The history of CVJs is interesting. A company that GKN acquired contained the CVJ technology and production processes. However, GKN executives discovered CVJ technology in the acquired firm only after the acquisition. The act of genius at GKN, then, was discovering CVJs and letting them drive the firm's strategy over the next thirty years.

Some might call this discovery of CVJs "luck." But GKN has gotten lucky in this way again and again throughout its history. Indeed, GKN always works very hard at being lucky. Take, for example, the period in the early 1980s when contract cancellations began to pose a real problem for GKN's businesses. Typically, the company would land a contract and then proceed to find the engineers necessary to staff that project. Unfortunately, customers would then often postpone or cancel these contracts, keeping engineers unemployed or idle until new work could be found for them. To deal with this recurrent situation, GKN's units began to "rent out" the services of their engineers for short assignments—which created an inventory of engineering talent that was easy to manage and low cost. For their part, GKN executives could pull the engineers back into the organization whenever needed. The units started the practice on an informal basis, but it proved so successful that GKN—to further its profitable growth strategy—created a new division to manage the hiring out of its own and other engineers on short-term contracts.

The result? GKN recombined its reputation for attracting topflight engineers as well as its talent for developing engineering skills and its extensive network of contacts to start what was, for all intents and purposes, a highly sophisticated employment agency. The new division, baptized with the name Engage, is now growing at breakneck speed. GKN executives had known the Engage business model for years. All they had to do was formalize this model, bring it under the umbrella of a new division, and recombine it with GKN's existing divisions.

Everything in Moderation, Including Moderation

I warned in the introduction to this book about the dangers of over-selling management techniques, resulting in unrealistic hopes that give way to fruitless management fads. It is important that I moderate certain claims, therefore, because I have painted a very rosy picture of change at GKN in order to exemplify creative recombination in the clearest and most forceful way possible.

So let's be clear. I am not claiming that GKN recombined every one, or even most, of its useful assets or recombinants. I discuss in the next chapter how, during a GKN engagement with one of its companies, Westland Helicopters, I witnessed its executives discover serendipitously a process that they successfully and virtually painlessly recombined with their existing processes. I know, however, that GKN was not always so lucky.

Nor am I saying that GKN brings about massive change without *any* creative destruction. It is true, for instance, that GKN founded Engage largely by recombining GKN's existing assets. It is also true, however, that Engage experienced growing pains—having to part with one of its early CEOs, for instance. So I am not making the overblown claim that GKN did not destroy anything, or that it brought about massive change without any pain.

What I am asserting, however, is that GKN taught me by its words and deeds that it is possible to tip the balance firmly toward creative recombination and away from creative destruction. Creative recombination, not destruction, can become the default to which leaders, managers, and employees turn first. Finally, what I am claiming is that GKN manages change in a way that brings it much closer to the change without pain ideal.

Why does the stress on recombination over destruction make changes cheaper, less painful, and more effective at GKN than in comparable companies? First, creative recombination enables the existing parts of GKN to continue operating as they are recombined, lessening the disruptive stopping and starting that is necessary if old parts have to be destroyed and new parts invented from scratch. Second, making smaller, incremental changes makes it unnecessary to take such radically destabilizing steps as obliterating large numbers of jobs and positions as GKN implements each recombination. Third, employees at

GKN are familiar with the preexisting parts that are recombined. Therefore, a change such as the GKN Engage launch is much less anxiety producing than if GKN had acquired a brand-new business or created one from scratch. Finally, the parts that GKN recombines, unlike transplanted parts, are native to GKN and less likely to be rejected, which would require yet more destabilizing change.

All kinds of locutions exist in the English language to describe how GKN goes about crafting changes: "making do with what you have," "using a little Yankee ingenuity," "pulling yourself up by your own bootstraps," "making a silk purse out of a sow's ear," "not throwing the baby out with the bath water." But clearly many other cultures also see the value of such creative recombination, including the French, whose word *bricolage* refers to the same kind of process in which one somehow "makes do" with what one already has lying around in order to create a functional collage of parts. The German *flickschusterei* has a similar connotation—"cobbling together," referring to a person who pieces together shoes using existing patches of leather. The Turkish *Bulup buluşturmak* also translates literally as finding and matching (or pulling together) in order to create a new outfit. The Japanese *kumikaeru,* or recombination, is used in the sense of genetic recombination. The British took the German word *klug* ("clever"), recombined it with an *e,* and gave us the English word *kluge* or *kludge*—defined in the dictionary as "any solution for accomplishing a task, especially mechanical, which consisted of various otherwise unrelated parts and mechanisms, cobbled together in a untidy or downright messy manner."[9]

The kind of change I'm talking about—whether you call it creative recombination, Yankee ingenuity, or tinkering or kludging in your basement—is one way to bring us closer to the change without pain ideal. To clarify, consider what creative recombination is not: Recombination is not an approach that involves obliterating the past to make way for some perceived notion of a brand-new future. Divorcing to remarry, gutting your house to rehabilitate it, downsizing your work force in order to rehire, and destroying the current organizational structure in order to restructure are so many examples of the latter approach. Often called creative destruction, that is precisely the kind of highly destabilizing change management process that gurus have overprescribed for several decades.

Creative Recombination Versus Creative Destruction

Although creative destruction can be inevitable in a world of excessive change, it should not be the default option. By wiping out the present and then having to reinvent the future, it is the change modality that has the greatest potential to create the highest degree of disruption and change-related pain.

Creative recombination, on the other hand, can be a much less wrenching process. As we have seen, rather than destroying parts of a company and inventing whole new structures, change comes through combining existing elements of a firm into new, more useful configurations. The printing press, to use an example of a technological recombination without which Harvard Business School Press could not have published my book, resulted from Gutenberg's recombination of the wine press and the coin-stamping machine. Had he instead relied on creative destruction—and in essence tried to invent a whole new kind of press and a never-before-seen stamping machine—old Gutenberg would probably have soon given up in frustration.

These recombinations stand in sharp contrast to the frustrating attempts at creative destruction that people in organizations undergo today. When firms make those attempts serially—as in our opening example of Cisco Systems—repetitive-change syndrome results, along with its symptoms: initiative overload, change-related chaos, and employee anxiety, cynicism, and burnout. Let us now examine creative destruction versus creative recombination in the workplace through the lens of each of these facets.

Initiative Overload Because creative destruction typically requires many more change initiatives than does creative recombination, it is more likely to cause initiative overload. With creative destruction, you have to first destroy what you've had in place, then design a new system, and then implement it—all of which is likely to create resistance in the organization. This means you then have to take yet another step, which is to start the process all over again.

Take, for example, the case of Bank of America when its executive team decided to create a new organizational measurement system for the bank's lending function. Specifically, the team wanted to switch from measuring and rewarding the number of loans the bank processed to measuring the profitability of those loans. To accomplish this, the bank applied creative destruction. In the end it met its goal—but not without an enormous amount of time, effort, and much pain all around.

Why? Because the creative destruction required at least four major types of change initiatives. First, Bank of America had to obliterate the current system, which meant that employees had to abandon and unlearn that system. Second, the bank had to blueprint a fresh system, devising the new measures and aligning them with the new measurement structures. Third, it had to build the blueprint, which meant designing the actual loan measures and who would receive them, how frequently, with what feedback and rewards, and so on.

Finally, the bank had to put in place what it built so that it was understood and accepted by those people—primarily loan officers—who would be measured, guided, and rewarded by that system. This meant actually implementing the measurement system so that people knew how to develop and code the data, understood the new measurement's purpose and consequences, and felt that the measures were useful and helpful and were therefore aligned with them.

That way of creating change proved as difficult as it sounds. The then CEO, Tom Clausen in a talk at Columbia University, tells a story of how, many months into the change initiative, he visited all of the bank's loan officers. When he asked them, "Making any money on those loans?" the reply he received, inevitably, was: "Great! I'm making more loans than ever." No mention whatsoever of how profitable those loans were. The new measurement system had been announced, all of the steps chronicled previously had been taken—and yet at that point there was still no real buy-in to the new measurement system. It was simply too complex, involving too many change initiatives along the way, for people to respond well. It was not until many, many months later, after asking the "loan profitability question" to hundreds of employees that, in the words of Clausen, "the bastards finally understood I was serious about profitability." [10] Clausen's use of the "b" expletive to refer to his Bank of America employees only underscores the highly destabilizing nature of such changes.

Now consider how part of a large railroad, Deutsche Bahn, used creative recombination to achieve such a measurement change in a mere two steps. First, the countless measures that were in use throughout the firm were inventoried and classified into four categories. Second, eighteen existing measures spanning the four categories were retained, while the others were eliminated. That was it. Creative recombination involved only inventorying existing parts—measures, in this instance—and recombining them. The old measurement system did not have to be completely obliterated. Moreover, new measurements did not have to be designed, created, and tested. Rather, the task was to find and leverage existing measures that were right for this firm (those which, anyhow, were really being used). The firm simply needed to put to a new use what it already had and to do more of what it already did well.

Recombination requires fewer initiatives for two additional reasons. First, recombination minimizes the need to reinvent the wheel because the process begins by looking around to find if a wheel already exists that can be reused, redeployed, and recombined. Second, creative recombination minimizes the potential for pendulum swings between mutually exclusive alternatives, such as centralization and decentralization, in-sourcing and outsourcing, or product and functional organizational designs. The recombination process begins not just with looking at what current parts of the organization you can recombine, but also at what past elements you can revive, redeploy, reuse, and recombine. The process, therefore, brings squarely into focus any mutually exclusive alternative solutions that were already tried in the past.

Change-Related Chaos Because creative destruction involves a transition period between the time when change agents destroy the old system and when they finish implementing the new system, it tends to create elevated levels of change-related chaos. During this often protracted in-between period, the firm can be both literally and figuratively out of control.

Such was the case in the classic example of Citibank in the 1970s, when John Reed, the CEO-to-be of what was to become Citigroup, experimented with sweeping, rapid changes in business processes.[11] His goal was to transform radically an old back-office check-processing operation into a highly efficient financial services system. He shut down operations on Friday, September 2, 1971. By Saturday, the bank had eliminated existing processes. By Sunday it had replaced them with the new processes. By Monday, the bank had thrown the switch on the reengineered checking-processing system.

But by the end of that week, it was apparent that the new check-processing center was, indeed, self-destructing. The paper pipeline had erupted, and unprocessed documents were accumulating. By the end of the second week Citibank's money pipeline had burst. Why did Citibank's change fail so spectacularly? Because although existing processes had been destroyed on Friday, when the switch was thrown on Monday the new processes had not yet been fully tested and implemented. In the end, it became apparent to everyone that the change process had wreaked such chaos that it was almost destined to fail.

The Citibank case occurred in the 1970s, but it was really no different from what happened at thousands of firms in the 1990s that underwent the business process reengineering (BPR) advised by Michael Hammer—and failed spectacularly as well.[12] (We will examine that fad and its consequences in chapter 6.)

Creative recombination, on the other hand—unlike BPR and the Citibank change initiative of the 1970s—requires much less of a transition period and therefore less chaos. Because the recombinants already exist, you spend less time breaking down old parts and inventing and implementing new ones. Often recombinants can even continue operating for the duration of the change. When Deutsche Bahn changed its measurement system, the eighteen kinds of measures that it retained never stopped functioning. Throughout the transition, the railroad continued to use them to collect, process, and disseminate information.

Creative recombination also tends to generate less change-related political chaos. Indeed, because little is destroyed, there is less to have to defend or justify within the firm. Managers spend less time and energy protecting their jobs, skill base, or authority. Moreover, NIH—"not invented here" syndrome—becomes less of an issue. People typically do not reject as "foreign inventions" change initiatives that recombine already existing organizational components.

Employee Cynicism H. L. Mencken once said "a cynic is a man that when he smells flowers looks around for a coffin." The levels of employee cynicism, anxiety, and burnout that result from creative destruction are well documented. Consider, for example, the merger between Chase and J.P. Morgan in 2000 and their attempt to create the single, massive firm called J.P. Morgan Chase. This was a classic case of creative destruction. For years, Chase had been chomping up firm after firm—Chemical Bank being only one example—which had created deep-seated problems of integration and employee alienation as Chase forced one change after another on its people. The J.P. Morgan merger, in which thousands of employees were funneled together to make one big company, triggered cynicism and anxiety in so many people that they left the newly merged firm en masse. One senior investment banker I spoke with told me that not long after the creation of J.P. Morgan Chase, she was the only person left of the 60 people who had once worked in her unit!

Creative recombination, on the other hand, tends to be much less disruptive for employees—in large part because there is less initiative overload and less change-related chaos. Because employees aren't continually wasting effort reinventing the wheel or swinging on a pendulum between extremes of change, they don't become so cynical. Because recombinants are not new and unfamiliar, employee anxiety stays at bay. And because recombinatory change requires less work in general than destructive change, people tend not to burn out.

Outline of the Book

This chapter and the next describe creative recombination. The following seven chapters demonstrate how to creatively recombine various elements of your organization, as well as how to recombine elements *outside* your organization.

More specifically, chapters 3 through 7 explore different dimensions of the organization and how to apply creative recombination. Chapter 3 looks at *people* and how to avoid downsizing by redeploying the talent companies already have. Chapter 4 examines the organization's *social networks* and how, instead of creating yet another new information technology network, companies can leverage social networks in order to reach for painless change. Chapter 5 looks at *culture* and ways that an organization can revive its values, rather than trying to invent them from scratch. Chapter 6 explores *processes*—specifically, how to salvage good processes rather than reengineer them. Similarly, chapter 7 looks at organizational *structure* with an eye toward reusing its parts instead of going through the painful process of replacing and reorganizing them altogether.

Each of these chapters focuses on how to recombine one or more elements from within the firm—people, networks, culture, processes, and structure. Chapter 8 switches the focus from recombinants originating inside the firm to those originating outside the firm. It examines how to effect large-scale change involving not only a firm's recombinants but also those belonging to its suppliers, its customers, and even its competitors.

Chapter 9 turns to the question of *when* to recombine. More specifically, it challenges the notion of continuous change—whether by creative destruction or creative recombination—and introduces a technique for balancing stability and change to reduce change-related pain. This technique, pacing, alternates periods of stability and change, counterbalancing one with the other to exploit the benefits of both. Chapter 10 concludes the book with some practical tips for keeping your company's "recombinant muscles" limber and thereby pursuing change without pain as an ideal over the lifetime of the organization.

Finally, I have placed materials pertinent to the book on a Web site—www.ChangeWithoutPain.com. I hope that ChangeWithoutPain.com will become a bit of a Web-based basement workshop. In it, you will find Web tools; links to articles, stories, and examples; and a threaded discussion group. I will post not only my recombinants, but any and all forms of recombinants that readers of this book might want to contribute for others to recombine.

The Change Without Pain Ideal

The prominent behavioral scientist Kurt Lewin once said, "There can be no change without pain."[13] Or, to put it more succinctly, "No pain, no change." Although I agree wholeheartedly with the truth behind that saying, I would also add three important caveats. First, in the current environment of excessive change, it is important not to overgeneralize. Yes, sometimes no pain means no change, but sometimes excessive levels of change-related pain can also render change slower, more expensive, and much more likely to fail entirely. In other words: More pain, less change. We must entertain the real possibility, therefore, that less pain equals more change.

Second, "No pain, no change" cannot be the standard against which we judge change management, because the phrase then becomes the excuse for every form of badly managed change. For example, "The organizational change succeeded, but the organization suffered unbearable pain and did not survive. Well, you know—no pain, no change."

Third, "No pain, no change" cannot remain the standard. Otherwise, it becomes the ready-made justification for why change is so difficult, for why so many change attempts fail, and for ever more change management fads.

This book proposes a different ideal to which to aspire: change without pain—that is, change that leaders and managers can repeat again and again without creating, over time, initiative overload, widespread change-related chaos, and employee cynicism and burnout. I advocate change without pain not because the mission of executives is to eliminate pain from organizational life (how boring and unchallenging work would become), but because in an environment of already excessive change, additional change-related pain impedes further change, raises its cost, and reduces its effectiveness. Change without pain is an ideal that, even if it is unachievable, will challenge and push people who develop advice about change management to craft better approaches to change itself.

In the next chapter, we begin to explore this notion of change without pain by looking more closely at how leaders and managers achieve it—namely, through the basic principles of creative recombination.

2   Creative Recombination

*T*HE SENIOR EXECUTIVE *team at Westland Helicopters—the largest division of GKN's Westland Aerospace—was suffering the turmoil of changing from a primary reliance on a mature military market to an additional reliance on a rapidly growing civilian market. The division's production runs had been extremely small, typically just four helicopters, each customized for a specific type of military mission—submarine hunting, for example, or tank busting. That production style was fine as long as military budgets were big. But after the end of the Cold War, the market became much more competitive, and the division came under intense pressure to achieve economies of scale in development and production. In other words, it needed to change.*

Change it did. Indeed, Westland Helicopters became awash in so many change initiatives that it had trouble getting helicopters out the door. It had trapped itself in a cycle of repetitive-change syndrome in which executives addressed problems created by one wave of creative destruction with yet another wave of creative destruction that only compounded the problem.

Blind to this vicious cycle, the overworked senior executives faced another change: launching yet another product-development change program to obliterate what was wrong with the existing program. Fortunately, the executive team was able to see that it could not continue to do its work while taking on more change management responsibility. Sick with repetitive-change syndrome, this crack team of highly committed executives agreed to try a new approach—resulting in a rare fairy-tale ending for a division so overwrought with change initiatives.

By looking around the division and its parent company to see what they already had in place that could be reused to craft the changes they needed, the executives found an easy, cost-efficient solution. First, they discovered that they already had a very good product-development model in the company's in-house software division. With a little customization and translation, they realized the process could be adapted to helicopter production and therefore minimize product design costs. Second, they could improve production economies by reusing the knowledge of employees who had come to the division from the automotive sector of the parent company and therefore already had experience with mass production of cars. Finally, they redeployed another product proposition that they called the "Barbie Doll," which had long been in use in another division of the company. This enabled them to build a base helicopter that could be dressed up (or recombined) with any number of accessories—guns, bombs, and avionics—for customers in the military to play with. The strategy allowed for mass production as well as mass customization, enabling the organization to reap economies of both scale and customization. Of course, the change was not pure creative recombination. Some creative destruction was necessary, but much less than had been the norm.

Unlike the highly disruptive and painful change modalities that typically accompany creative destruction, creative recombination facilitates the kind of smoother, easier, and more cost-efficient transformation that Westland Helicopters was able to foster in the end. The division did not need to obliterate the past to create the future: Few layoffs occurred, few new software or machines were purchased, few brand-new ideas were either invented or imported from outside, and little cultural shift was required. The overall effect? Westland Helicopters achieved much less destabilizing and painful change, with great success.

Change without pain, then, comes first by knowing what you already have that you could reuse in your organization (rather than creating, inventing, or purchasing something new) and second by knowing how you can reuse, redeploy, and recombine these existing elements of the firm into new configurations. That is creative recombination in action.

Let us now explore this notion in more detail by examining what specific kinds of things an organization might already have lying around its workshop with which it can work to effect positive, painless change.

What to Recombine

One of the key challenges in creative recombination has to do with the possibilities you see. Finding those organizational elements that you can recombine effectively begins by knowing first where to look. What follows is a *mapping technique* that highlights the full range of possibilities and acts as a tool to make sure you don't miss any good ones.

The Five Recombinants

Look at any organizational architecture and you'll find five common elements, or *recombinants:* people, networks, culture, processes, and structure. These are the organizational equivalents of the steel rods, old leather belts, and metal disks found lying around my father's workshop and with which he crafted my potter's wheel. Put another way, they are the things you'll find sitting right in your own corporate basement: They are the organizational elements that you can recombine to create painless change.

The people in your organization, of course, are your employees. These employees create networks among one another; that is, they exchange information, favors, resources, and even gossip through the firm's informal systems. The firm's culture comprises its values (for instance, decision by consensus), norms (what the firm considers normal behavior, such as working past midnight on weekends), and informal roles (becoming an informal mentor, for instance). Processes are the recurrent activities—such as purchasing, production, or distribution—that enable a firm to transform inputs such as raw material, labor, or capital into outputs such as products or services. Structure refers to the organizational boxes, lines of communication and reporting, staffing, and control mechanisms that managers put in place to make sure that employees carry out processes effectively and efficiently. Thus, selling is a process, whereas a sales bonus is a structural control mechanism to guarantee effective and efficient sales.

When you craft change through creative recombination, rather than eliminating existing people, networks, culture, processes, and structure and replacing them with new ones, you instead work with what you already have. In other words, you look only at existing parts of the organizational architecture for your change solutions.

The shrewdness of the leaders at Westland Helicopters was evidenced not so much by the fact that they figured out how to mass produce helicopters, but by the fact that they saw what they could recombine to do so. They discerned two existing elements in their processes—a software development process and the Barbie Doll process—that might be useful, as well as the invaluable automotive industry knowledge that some of their people possessed. And they saw that they could recombine these elements to create a production line that could generate hundreds of helicopters at a time, rather than batches of only three or four. In so doing, the executives also revived yet another organizational recombinant—a forgotten value, latent in Westland Helicopters' culture, for "making do with what we have."

The result was that Westland Helicopters crafted a painless, cost-efficient change by creatively recombining processes, people, and an aspect of its culture. Imagine how much time, effort, and money the division would have wasted—not to mention the disruption created—had the executive team continued to invent "new" solutions to its problems rather than leveraging its existing recombinants!

Another way of thinking of the five recombinants is as a structure of Legos, atoms, or Tinker Toys—those multicolored plastic hubs with holes that can be linked together by plastic spokes to create all forms of combinations and configurations. Change in a Lego or Tinker Toy structure does not have to take place by creative destruction—ripping the entire structure apart, throwing away all the pieces, buying a new set, and rebuilding an entirely different structure. Rather, change takes place by tinkering—taking one block from one substructure and adding it to another. In still other instances, entire Lego substructures can be recombined with other substructures and can play a new role in the overall structure.

Figure 2-1 depicts the organizational Legos: people, culture, network, process, and structure recombinants. It also illustrates how the five recombinants tend to divide along the lines of a "hard axis" and "soft axis" and how they overlap when a company, such as Westland

FIGURE 2-1

The Recombinant Map

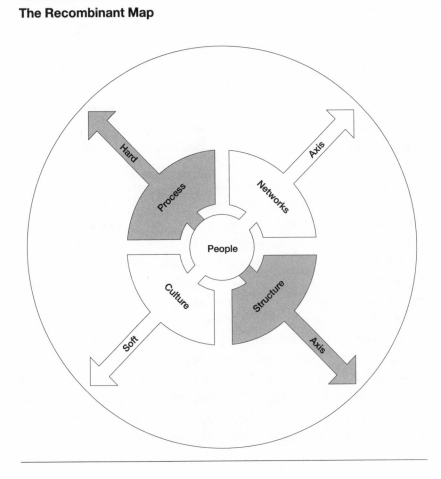

Helicopters, changes through creative recombination. The process–structure axis represents the "hard" organizational recombinants axis—that is, recombinants directly under the control of management. At Westland Helicopters, this was helicopter acquisition, production, and contracting processes, as well as the elaborate division of labor into coordinated production units. These processes were reinforced by measurement, evaluation, and rewards systems that guaranteed that each attack helicopter was delivered on schedule, with the right armament and battle-worthy qualities necessary to defeat the enemy. The network–culture axis represents the "soft" organizational recombinants axis, because recombinants such as culture and networks often tend to emerge in an unplanned fashion within an organization rather than being directly dictated by the management team. At Westland Helicopters, these soft elements included the firm's engineering culture, which valued producing fast, elegant, and lethal military helicopters rather than a better widget, and extensive social networks linking not only employees with the firm, but also some of these employees with regulators, army and air force generals, and all forms of technical specialists outside the firm.

Every time a firm pursues an existing or new strategy by reusing, redeploying, or recombining aspects of its people, networks, culture, structures, or processes—rather than destroying them and recreating them from scratch—the firm is creatively recombining. So instead of downsizing, redeploy your people's talents. Rather than paying for some new form of computer network to manage the firm's knowledge assets, leverage the social networks through which this knowledge is already flowing. Instead of inventing a whole new culture, turn to cultural values already present in the firm and revive or reinforce them. Rather than restructuring, reuse existing elements found in your present structure. And rather than reengineering brand-new processes, salvage perfectly good ones that have long been used in the organization.

In short, you do not start with a clean white sheet of paper and design your ideal vision from scratch. You do not slash and burn what exists in order to create the Promised Land. You start with what you already have lying around in the corporate basement. Then you use good old Yankee ingenuity, tinkering, *bricolage, bulup buluşturmak, kumikaeru,* and *flickschusterei* to futz, fiddle, jury-rig, bootstrap, cobble together, and patch your way to effective change that causes the least disturbance to everyone.

But let's take a step back for a moment. Once leaders have used mapping techniques and know what to look for—which type of elements in the organization they want to reuse, redeploy, or recombine—they might wonder what the trick is for finding useful ones. In other words, they need a *search technique* in addition to the mapping technique.

One search technique is to ask, "What do I need in order to produce my desired end?" and then go about looking for those means in the organization. At Westland Helicopters, for example, the executive team began by clarifying the end they needed to pursue: to move from batch producing to mass producing helicopters. That clarity and focus enabled them to discover what organizational recombinants they possessed could serve as means to this end—and became a key early step to finding the means to painless change.

The other search technique is to ask, "What do I already have lying around in my basement, and what emergent opportunities can I capitalize on?" The task then is to find a good end to which to put those existing means. Let us look at this means and ends question in more detail.

Finding Recombinants

Ask most people, "How are problems solved or opportunities exploited?" and they will tell you in no uncertain terms that problems or opportunities occur first and that only subsequently do people find solutions to solve these problems or exploit these opportunities. Much more rarely will they recognize that solutions often emerge first and only then reveal heretofore unknown problems that these solutions can solve, or unknown opportunities they can serve to exploit. Recent advances in plastic surgery, for example, make it possible to modify the appearance of a person's navel. This solution is leading a growing number of people to discover a new problem in their appearance: their horrendously ugly "inny" or "outy." More pertinently, it was not until techniques were developed to describe a company's culture and to transform it that many CEOs realized that they had a "cultural problem" or a "cultural opportunity" in their firm.

Whether a solution is found to solve a problem by creating a means to an end or whether it serves to reveal an opportunity by creating ends for that means, the final result is the same: A means–end relationship is established and the problem is solved. So why, you might ask, bother dwelling on this distinction? Because the search techniques that resolve means-to-ends issues and ends-for-means issues are often extremely different.

Reconsider for a moment a basement workshop. One type of search technique is involved when a concrete problem or opportunity presents itself—for example, a child wants a potter's wheel, causing his father to go rummaging through discarded parts to find those necessary to create the wheel. The search technique is very different when recombiners go to the workshop with no particular problem in mind and look around for a set of parts with which they could build something useful.

In the case of Westland Helicopters, we saw how clarifying the ends helped those executives discover recombinants that could serve as means to those ends. Dow Corning, on the other hand, provides an example of how a company began with existing means and found ends that those means could serve. It had a process for turning plastic into thin, sticky, flexible sheets used in industrial coating applications. What other ends could this process serve? Answer: Saran Wrap, a multimillion dollar mass-market product. Good recombiners, then, can take an existing recombinant and search for new ends to which it could be applied.

The search for new ends for existing means is not another version of the mantra "build it and they will come." It implies, rather, that if you have already built it, why not find more ways for them to come? Indeed, we have known for a long time that the failure to exploit innovations is probably much more prevalent than the failure to innovate. Take the example of the Xerox PARC R&D facility. It invented, among other things, the mouse and the desktop computer graphical user interface. Xerox never commercialized these blockbuster innovations, leaving it to other companies to use these means to create brilliant products—companies such as Apple and Microsoft, who recombined Xerox's inventions with their own products.

Once you have framed your problem or opportunity and have decided which recombinants in your organization you will focus on, the next step is to know how you can bring together what you have in order to enact painless, cost-efficient change. In other words, you need to look at what I call the *action technique* that will enable you to most effectively reuse, redeploy, and recombine existing elements of the firm into new configurations.

How to Recombine

Mastering creative recombination comes from understanding the diversity of techniques that leaders, managers, and employees can utilize. Just as there is more than one search technique for deciding what and how much to recombine, so too there are a variety of action techniques for figuring out how best to recombine.

Many great change solutions fail not so much because they are the wrong ones but because change agents implement them poorly. Success depends on using the right action technique for each type of recombinant and supporting it with the right resources.

You can effect change through creative recombination by choosing among three very different action techniques, which I call *cloning, customizing,* and *translating.* Which action technique you choose depends on whether you're talking about recombining certain characteristics of people, networks, culture, processes, or structures. Each action technique requires not only different types of implementation processes but also different types of supporting knowledge in order to implement it properly.

Cloning

Of the three action techniques, cloning is the least arduous. Essentially, you just "plug and play"—as long as what you are cloning is completely compatible with the new environment in which it will be used. For example, most computer programs can be copied exactly and installed easily across standardized information technology (IT) platforms.

Clonable recombinants, or *clones* for short, are recombinants that have the same kinds of properties that such IT programs do—that is, the same means can be used, unmodified, to achieve the same ends successfully in a different part of the firm. Another example of a clonable recombinant might be a common return policy that you can implement across different franchised businesses and allow a percentage of returns within a particular range, regardless of the socioeconomic profile of each franchise's customers.

In our example of Westland Helicopters, the cultural value that the division instilled during its change program—the value of "making do with what we have"—was actually cloned and revived from a long-lost tradition within the division. During the years when relentless change by creative destruction was the mantra, that value had simply gone underground, replaced with "making do with the bold new visions and consultants we have." But the latent value of ingenious self-reliance did not die out entirely. As one engineer had told me, no two helicopters that the division built were ever the same and thus there always remained a need to "make do" and to jury-rig some improvised solution with existing parts and patches. Also, relentless change had caused so much disruption in routine operations that fire fighting—rapidly improvising solutions to put out burning problems—had risen to a fine art at Westland Helicopters. Fire fighting had bred a generation of highly skilled workers, recombination Michelangelos who could on a moment's notice put together from mismatched parts beautiful solutions to avert catastrophe. The "making do with what we have" value thus lived on in this firm, waiting to be revived at a moment's notice, cloned, and exploited by canny leaders.

It's important to remember, however, that not all elements of an organization can be cloned. The key to cloning, then, is first to know what you have that is clonable. Some recombinants on the soft axis of an organization, such as people, cannot be cloned (yet) for obvious reasons (although their skills and knowledge usually can be cloned in some way). Neither can certain social networks, because the social links binding people across the network rest on a hard-to-duplicate level of trust and cooperation. Even some recombinants on the hard axis of processes and structures are not clonable, although there exist many that can be.

For example, the GKN Meineke automotive franchise developed a Web-based course for training some franchisees. It discovered that it could then roll out the course, unmodified, across not only most of its new franchises, but also its existing ones as well. An investment bank I worked with, on the contrary, found out that to move a Web course reinforcing the company's values of integrity and customer focus from the United States to the United Kingdom required extensive changes to fit the U.K. context. That's why, when you think of cloning, it's important first to know what you're dealing with.

Customizing

Change agents cannot simply clone certain recombinants, but must rather customize them in order to recombine them and bring about change. They must alter them to fit different areas in an organization. Or, put differently, you must modify the means to achieve the same ends successfully across parts of your firm.

At Westland Helicopters, when the executives redeployed the mass production know-how and skills of their people with auto industry expertise, they were not using those people in exactly the same way they had been used in the auto industry. The executives had to customize the know-how to the production of helicopters, with their greater technological complexity and flight security imperatives.

When you customize, then, you essentially must "refit and use." In that way, customizing is more challenging than cloning because it requires not only that you know what you are recombining, but also that you know why, how, and when the recombinant works.

For example, consider transferring to an American the skill of a Parisian driver—that is, the ability to get to any location in the mazelike city on time without either becoming hopelessly lost or being arrested. Such a skill transfer requires much more than handing the American a *Plan de Paris* mapping the fastest routes through the city. What is necessary is not just explicit information, such as "Take Avenue du Maine and turn on Boulevard Montparnasse." You also need more tacit information, such as "If it's a Friday and the weather is sunny, use an alternate route than the one on the map, because every other Frenchman will be following the same map. Unless, of course, it is August, and only foreigners occupy the road, in which case you can drive in a more universally aggressive and rude way. But only on streets other than the overcrowded streets—those listed in popular foreign guides to Paris."

In sum, what is necessary in transferring Parisian driving skills is not just "know-what" (i.e., what road to follow) but also "know-when" (i.e., when to use one route or another) and "know-how" (i.e., when to drive by Parisian standards and when to be more universally aggres-sive). Finally, and most important, is "know why"—that is, knowledge about why particular know-when and know-how are successful only under certain conditions.

Why is know-why so important? We know only that the recombi-nant—in this case, the path to get quickly from point A to point B in Paris—worked in one context. We have no theory of if, when, and how it works in other contexts. So we run the risk of using it wrongly in the right context, rightly in the wrong context, or worse, wrongly in the wrong context.

Disney, for example, tried to clone its Disney theme park formula in a location immediately outside Paris. What it lacked, however, was a careful understanding of why and how Disney theme parks work so well in the United States and Japan and why they would not work, uncustomized, in a European context. The result? Fiercely nationalistic French intellectuals dubbed Euro Disney a "cultural Chernobyl," French employees at Euro Disney rebelled at the rules dictating what type of undergarment they could wear, and French moms and dads searched fruitlessly for the obligatory glass of wine to accompany lunch.

Disney, to its credit, has been a masterful recombiner in almost every context save for Euro Disney. Not surprisingly, it quickly realized its mistake and with a little know-why, know-when, and know-how turned Euro Disney from a disastrous clone to a highly successful cus-tomization of the Disney theme park template.

Translating

Certain recombinants are essentially incompatible with new contexts. You therefore might need to translate them somehow to help them recombine more successfully and painlessly. In other words, you need to interpret, reinvent, and render them useful in the new situation. The recombinants thereby achieve the same ends in an organization, but by completely different means. Forks, chopsticks, and right hands, for instance, are translations of different means for the same end—eating. Likewise, the corporate cultural value of timeliness may have to be reinvented when it is used in a country like the United States, where "time is money" and therefore timeliness is valued, as opposed to its use in a country like Spain, where how time is spent is valued over how much time is spent. (For instance, skipping the customary long, leisurely lunch, even in business contexts, would be thought strange indeed.)

At Westland Helicopters, although the executives leveraged and customized skills in their employees with automotive expertise to fit helicopter production, they had to translate other recombinants before they would work correctly. Most people would agree, for instance, that a piece of software is very different from a helicopter. When the executives redeployed development processes from their software to their helicopter operations, they were not simply cloning or even customizing the processes. Rather, they were copying the functions served by each step in the software development process, not these steps themselves, to develop helicopters. Likewise, some Euro Disney features had to be translated for the European context—for example, a lunchtime menu without beer and wine had to be translated into one with both prominently featured.

Successful translations are thus the most difficult of all the techniques for implementing the kind of recombination that facilitates change without pain. Translations generally require face-to-face dialogue with people who have used the recombinant successfully in another context and can explain how it functions to reach certain ends.

For example, the consultants at top firms such as McKinsey, Booz•Allen & Hamilton, or ATKearny are masters at recombining the experience they develop in one consulting engagement to solve similar problems encountered in another. The consulting problems they face are so complex and ambiguous, and the standards of excellence they are held to are so high, that recombining methods developed in one engagement requires much more than cloning or customization. The methods they use, therefore, serve as sources of inspiration for translating a particular method from one consulting job to another to achieve the same ends.

When face-to-face (or phone-to-phone) dialogue becomes necessary to obtain the information needed to translate a technique used in one consulting engagement to the next, another type of knowledge becomes crucial: knowledge about who to contact to have such a dialogue. I call this knowledge *know-who*. Moreover, if you lack know-who, it is also crucial to know of those rare individuals, or IT systems, which can put you in contact with the right people to talk with. I call this *know-who-knows-who* knowledge. Not surprisingly, rich interpersonal networks as well as world-class information technology provide this type of knowledge to consultants.

Table 2-1 offers an at-a-glance summary of the distinctive characteristics of all three action techniques and how they compare with one another. Now that we have examined the various action techniques that enable creative recombination, let us consider scale. Whether a particular change program is small or big can determine the particular approach used. Recombining a single type of recombinant, for

TABLE 2-1

Cloning, Customizing, and Translating

Type of Recombinant	Characteristics	Implementation Process	Supporting Resources	Example
Clonable	The same means will achieve the same ends successfully across parts of a firm	*Cloning:* Formalizing, transmitting, and adopting	*Know-what:* What is the recombinant to reuse?	E-mailing copies of a computer program and mandating its use across a firm with a common PC standard
Customizable	The means must be modified to achieve the same ends successfully across parts of a firm	*Customizing:* Communicating, adopting, and fitting	*Know-when, know-how, and know-why:* When, how, and why should the recombinant be reused?	Language training for specialists deployed in different national subsidiaries
Reinventable	The means must be reinvented to achieve the same ends successfully across parts of a firm	*Translating:* Interpreting, reinventing, and adopting	*Know-who:* Who knows what, why, and when about this recombinant? *Know-who-knows-who:* Who knows which people have the right know-what, know-when, and know-why for specific recombinants?	Recreating a corporate value or a brand print in one national subsidiary to reach the same end in the other subsidiary's national culture

instance, can usually be achieved by either cloning, customizing, or translating. Recombining many recombinants, however, is so complex that it can rarely be achieved with mere cloning, and usually requires the use of customizing or even translating.

As you work through the next chapters in this book, keep in mind that changing through creative recombination is not something that you can apply easily to the type of change-averse firms that we discussed in chapter 1. These are the old, stodgy, change-averse companies that have changed too little and that are a dying breed today anyway, given the fever pitch of relentless-change programs and the popularity of creative destruction in the last decades. The problem plaguing change-averse firms is that because of their excessive stability, over time they've become better and better at less and less until they are excellent at almost nothing—and are left with little to recombine. Rather, creative recombination applies to firms that have (or are about to have) changed too much—what I've called changeaholics—and are full of recombinants that they can leverage by reusing, redeploying, or reviving them for painless, cost-effective change.

Keep in mind too that although change by creative recombination is much less disruptive than change by creative destruction, it is disruptive nonetheless. When the firm should change and when it should stabilize its operations is an extremely important question that I turn to in chapter 9, where I examine the technique of pacing—counterbalancing periods of stability and change to exploit the benefits of both.

What You See Is What You Can Recombine

An old joke tells of a man who, walking down the street on his way to his night job, spots a drunk searching for something under a lamp post. Being a Good Samaritan, he asks the drunk what he is looking for. "My keys!" he answers in a loud, threatening tone. The Good Samaritan moves on. Hours later, as he is walking back from work, the streets still bathed in darkness, he spots the same drunk under the same lamp post, looking for the same set of keys. Because the drunk has sobered up a bit, the Good Samaritan asks the drunk why he is still looking for the keys in the same spot. The drunk answers in the same loud and threatening tone, "Because this is the only spot where there is enough light for me to find them!"

The joke is mediocre, but it makes an important point. A map, like the lamp post, tends to cast light on certain features of situations and to obscure others. However, what lies off the map, shrouded in darkness, may be what really matters. A good map or mapping technique for a particular purpose, therefore, helps us see certain courses of action and keeps us in the dark only about what does not matter. To travel from New York to Washington, for instance, a good large-scale road map need only reveal important highways, roads, and big cities. There are always smaller-scale maps to reveal every small road, one-way street, and alley necessary to find a specific address within big cities. Bad maps lack focus. They either focus on too much and overwhelm us with their complexity, or on not enough and keep us in the dark.

Likewise, if you hope to effect change through creative recombination, you need a good map to find the needed recombinants in the rich workshop of your organization and to figure out how to reuse, redeploy, or revive them. The rest of this book endeavors to do just that: provide a map that shows you how to implement creative recombination among specific recombinants in order to craft lasting change, painlessly and cost-effectively.

What is a good recombination map? First, it must cast light on where to look for the full range of recombinants, not just the obvious ones. Second, it must distinguish different types of recombinants. Third, it should show the kind of technique required when working with each type of recombinant. This chapter, for example, distinguished three action techniques for recombining that imply three types of recombinants: clonable (which can be copied and recombined), customizable (which can be copied but have to be modified in order to be recombined), and translatable recombinants (which cannot be copied, and must be translated in order to achieve the same ends and be recombined). The typology is useful because each type of recombinant requires a different recombination technique.

The next chapter examines how you can creatively recombine your people—or more accurately, particular strengths your people have. First, it examines what types of strengths people have. Second, it explores how to look for people with the strengths necessary to address a particular problem or opportunity and how to look for problems or opportunities that could be addressed with the strengths of the people we have. Third, it turns to how these strengths—when they have been found—can be recombined. It looks at which technique or techniques (cloning, customizing, or translating) can be used most effectively and under what circumstances. Finally, it provides a series of examples of the ingenious tactics used by firms to recombine their people rather than downsize them.

Subsequent chapters look in turn at creating change without pain through the other four recombinants of organizational networks, cultures, structures, and processes. Each of these chapters has the same four-part structure as chapter 3: a look first at mapping techniques that reveal what aspects of the particular recombinant you can reuse, redeploy, and recombine; followed by search techniques necessary to find such recombinants in a concrete situation; and then by action techniques—that is, techniques for cloning, customizing, or translating a particular type of recombinant. The final part of each chapter brings the argument down to desk-level decisions. This part answers the question "OK, how do I put these techniques into practice in my firm?" by providing a wide range of examples of firms that have done so.

Let us begin our look at implementing creative recombination by examining what is probably any firm's most valuable recombinant: its people. If organizations truly wish to leave behind the days of creative destruction and the painful aspects of repetitive-change syndrome that such destruction engenders, there is no better place to start. The change without pain ideal, after all, is a quintessentially human and humane ideal.

3   Redeploying Talent Rather Than Downsizing

I WAS TEACHING *a class of executive M.B.A.'s,
students with ten or more years of managerial
experience. We were discussing downsizing. John,
by far and above the class leader, declared, "I am at Columbia
Business School because of a downsizing. [Laughter from the
class] I wasn't fired, I just quit." He proceeded to tell us the
story of his firm, a large U.S. consumer products firm whose
name he wants to remain off the record. When the firm's CEO
decided to downsize his organization, he started with his own
leadership team—firing them one by one until two-thirds of his
top lieutenants remained. He then instructed each of those lieutenants to fire one-third of his or her subordinates. The remaining two-thirds at that level, in turn, were instructed to fire one-
third of their subordinates, and so on, all the way down the line.*

For the people in the firm, the downsizing process became a slow, excruciating death march as each managerial layer had to complete its layoffs before those at the next level down could begin. John says that "it was like watching a heavy piano crash slowly through each floor of a high rise building—and at each level, people had to decide where they should stand to avoid being crushed." Indeed, as the firings trickled down the hierarchy, the game became to align oneself with those who were less likely to be fired—and who had bosses who were less likely to be fired. So when someone was unexpectedly fired eight levels up the hierarchy, there was a mad rush to realign at every level below.

The protracted stress of organizational politics, disruptions in the chain of command, and the threat of being fired came close to grinding the entire firm to a halt. Eventually, the process became so exceedingly painful, disruptive, and politicized that star employees like John opted on their own to leave the firm, in total disgust.

The downsizing fad of the late 1980s and mid-1990s was perhaps one of the most obvious and widespread periods of creative destruction that the corporate world had ever seen. During that time, more than 90 percent of large firms across Canada, France, Germany, Great Britain, and the United States strategically laid off hundreds of thousands of employees, and in excess of two-thirds of these firms would downsize yet again.[1] Some of these downsizings were necessary, since the market had shifted drastically and rapidly, leaving virtually no choice for poorly performing firms but to lay off workers. However, a clear pattern of empirical evidence indicates that fewer than half of the firms that downsized in the 1980s experienced the profit or productivity growth they'd hoped the layoffs would bring, and at the end of the decade their stock prices lagged industry averages.

For some kinds of organizations, the effects of downsizing were even more severe, becoming literally a matter of life and death. In one study of 281 acute care hospitals, for instance, mortality and morbidity rates were between 200 percent and 400 percent higher in those hospitals that downsized.[2] Moreover, the immediate costs savings associated with downsizing that these hospitals enjoyed disappeared within one to one and a half years.

Across all kinds of organizations, the consequences of downsizing and its attendant creative destruction were severe. As we saw in the opening example of the large consumer firm that downsized by cutting one-third of its people at each organizational level, the effects included continual disruption in the chain of command that soon led to organizational paralysis and demotivation (and eventual mass exodus) of the firm's star performers. Multiple carefully conducted scientific studies have pointed to twenty specific problems associated with downsizing (table 3-1).

TABLE 3-1

Dysfunctional Consequences of Downsizing

1. Destruction of employee and customer trust and loyalty

2. Loss of personal relationships between employees and customers

3. Disruption of smooth, predictable routines in the firm

4. Increase in and formalization of rules, standardization, and rigidity

5. Decrease in creativity

6. Loss of interpersonal interactions over time, leading to decreased cross-unit and cross-level knowledge

7. Less documentation and therefore less sharing of information about changes

8. Loss of employee productivity

9. Loss of a common organizational culture

10. Loss of innovativeness

11. Increased resistance to change

12. Decreasing employee morale, commitment, and loyalty

13. Escalation of politicized special-interest groups and political infighting

14. Risk aversion and conservatism in decision making

15. Increased costs and redundancies

16. Increasing interpersonal conflict

17. Negative effects on the personal health of employees (e.g., increases in headaches, stomach problems, and elevated blood pressure, as well as reports of increased drinking and smoking)

Continued

TABLE 3 - 1 *(continued)*

Dysfunctional Consequences of Downsizing

18. Increases in negative psychological symptoms (e.g., anxiety, depression, insomnia, feelings of helplessness, cognitive difficulties)

19. Loss of self-esteem, loss of self-mastery, dissatisfaction with self, pessimism, power-lessness, and rigidity

20. Decreases in family cohesion, increases in conflict, decline in spouses' psychological well-being, increases in domestic arguments, deteriorating family climate, and a sevenfold increase in divorce and separation

Source: Kim S. Cameron, "Strategic Organizational Downsizing: An Extreme Case," *Research in Organizational Behavior* 20 (1998): 185–229.

Fortunately, as we already began to see in the first two chapters, there is an alternative to downsizing employees. There is another way to effect change besides creative destruction and repetitive-change syndrome. This chapter examines what you can reuse, redeploy, and recombine of your organization's most valuable recombinants—your people's talents and knowledge—to craft lasting change without pain.

What to Recombine

In the introduction to this book, I mentioned the classic change management cases—the type of case you find in many books, articles, and courses about change management. These are cases that many change leaders know well because authors, consultants, and professors have used (and perhaps overused) them. They therefore can be reused. I hope this book can help us recombine them with current thinking and reconsider them in a fresh new light.

Consider the classic case of Peter Browning at Continental White Cap (CWC), a division of the Continental Can Company. I have read the teaching notes that are distributed to professors who teach the case and have both taught it and seen it taught many times.[3] It exemplifies many of the principles discussed in this chapter about creatively recombining people, although case teachers—myself among them—frequently teach it as a case of creative destruction.

The case discusses CWC, which since its beginnings in the 1920s had been extremely successful in its niche market of producing closures for containers. In the mid-1980s, however, the environment began to change, with increasing price wars in the market and the introduction of plastic (rather than metal) bottle caps, which CWC had yet to develop. Some of its oldest clients, such as H. J. Heinz (with which the division had been doing business since the 1940s), would soon have to take their business elsewhere because they were developing plastic squeeze bottles that would need plastic caps. But CWC didn't seem too concerned about any of these issues. In fact, given its long history of success, there was little perceived need, throughout CWC, to respond to the market changes at all. This was a happy, complacent division.

Enter Peter Browning, a new divisional vice president fresh from a brutal episode of downsizing at Bondware, another division of Continental Can. In his second turnaround assignment, corporate headquarters charged Peter Browning with helping CWC become more market focused, while reducing costs, increasing productivity, and maintaining sales performance. Time for another downsizing?

Not exactly. Browning began by looking around CWC's corporate basement. There he saw a number of very potent recombinants with which he could begin to effect change, most notably its people: a very skilled and extremely committed workforce that, historically, had been the source of the division's successes. Among other kinds of recombinations that Browning would ultimately make, he began his turnaround with a focus on reusing, redeploying, and recombining CWC's human assets.

Before we examine in more detail just how Peter Browning accomplished such sweeping change by recombining CWC's people, let's look at what kinds of recombinants an organization can find in its people that can be reused, redeployed, and recombined to foster its goals.

The People Recombinant Framework

We'll begin by looking at what aspects of people can best be recombined. After all, people, like diamonds, are multifaceted: The person is not really the recombinant, but rather his or her unique strengths are. The challenge becomes finding that diamond in the rough with the right talents, knowledge, skills, and so on that a leader can recombine in a particular situation to create painless change. What is needed, then, is a mapping framework that helps you decipher what recombinants to

FIGURE 3-1

The People Map

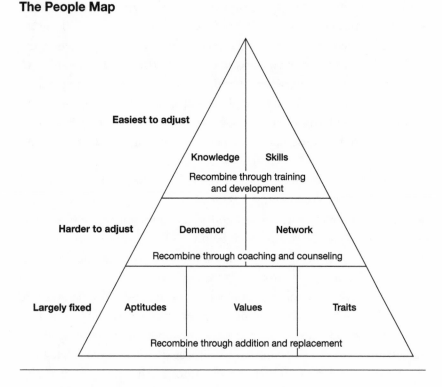

look for in people. Figure 3-1 is just such a tool. This framework, based on the work of Donald C. Hambrick, highlights what you already have in your employees that can be revived, reused, and redeployed—namely, their knowledge and skills; demeanors and networks; and values, aptitudes, and psychological traits.[4] I will illustrate these people recombinants shortly, through examples.

But first, why do the recombinants appear in a pyramid with three levels in the figure? Because a good map of individual characteristics that leaders and managers can recombine should not only reveal human diversity but should also distinguish those characteristics that leaders can easily modify and adjust from those that they can do little to alter—those toward the bottom of the pyramid. A good map should also suggest what techniques are appropriate—training, development, coaching, or counseling—for adjusting people's characteristics so that leaders and managers can successfully redeploy and recombine them with an existing position.

Let's return to the CWC example to illustrate this framework. Given that Peter Browning was charged with making CWC more market driven (in particular, able to compete in price wars and to cater to the new trend in plastics), the head of marketing would be key to any change plan. But Browning soon learned that the head of marketing, Jim Stark, lacked the aptitude to be a very effective manager of his sales force, and he wasn't addressing the new issues in the competitive environment. Browning would have to find someone else to head this critical function.

Fortunately, Stark had certain key strengths that Browning could leverage in order to redeploy him in a different part of the division. As Browning put it, "He was in the wrong job and we were not properly using his skills."[5] So rather than fire him, Browning gave Stark the job of director of package development and charged him with becoming a liaison with plastic container manufacturers. The result? Within two years Stark turned plastics into a competitive strength for the division, securing agreements with every major plastics manufacturer and earning a nice bonus for himself in the process. Looking at Stark through the lens of the people recombinant framework helps explain why Browning could recombine Stark, and why not doing so would have represented a tremendous lost opportunity.

Knowledge and Skills Consider the top of the pyramid: Knowledge is what you know, and skills are what you know how to do. Stark lacked much of the knowledge and skills necessary to liaise with plastic container manufacturers, but knowledge and skills are relatively easy to change. All it took, in the case of Stark, was a crash course in plastics.

Demeanor and Networks More difficult to alter than knowledge and skills are the recombinants appearing on the second level of our pyramid framework: demeanor and networks. Usually coaching or counseling offers a longer-term solution. The demeanor of an employee is the impression or perception that she or he creates in other people's minds. A person's demeanor develops slowly through childhood and life experiences. Once developed, moreover, other people expect it of that person. Otherwise, they appear out of role. So the people we know consistently reinforce our demeanor in every interaction we have with them. As a result, demeanor is much harder to change than many skills and areas of knowledge. It involves not only changing the person, but also changing his or her relation with other people, and maybe these people themselves. Luckily, Stark had the right demeanor for his new role.

Your personal network is everyone you know or knew, as well as everyone who knows or has known you. The networker's motto is, "It's not what you know, it's who you know." In other words, networkers know full well that their personal network contacts can be vital to getting their job done. Suffice it to say here that Jim Stark was no networker. He did not have a network of contacts among plastic container manufacturers that he could reuse and recombine to make the change to his new liaison role with these manufacturers. This presented a problem. It is difficult to change a person's network. Networking is not just meeting more people; it is also a process of building trust with people in your network. In the case of Jim Stark at CWC, developing his network to include executives at plastic container manufacturers necessitated that Stark be introduced to these executives by people at CWC who they trusted and who could vouch for Stark's expertise and trustworthiness. Normally, however, changing a person's networks may require not just introductions but also coaching and mentoring. Change tends to be slower and more gradual for the individual involved.

Values, Aptitudes, and Psychology People recombinants in the bottom portion of the pyramid are generally fixed, hardwired, and very hard to alter. Therefore, you should probably not attempt to recombine employees who lack the right aptitude, values, or psychological traits. No amount of coaching can instill certain characteristics into employees. No amount of training will create an aptitude for math, will change a deeply held personal value, or will turn a deeply introverted individual into an all-out, extroverted, wild and crazy guy.

Stark, however, like many employees at CWC, had tremendous personal values of loyalty to his firm. More important, like many people who rise to the top of their sales organizations, Stark had the psychological profile and aptitude to sell people, so to speak. These characteristics made him capable of selling CWC very effectively to plastic manufacturers. Downsizing Stark and replacing him with another person, therefore, would have meant an extended search for a person with the right aptitudes, values, and psychological traits to liaise with plastic manufacturers. The less painful route was to give Stark a crash course in plastics, give him entrée to the network of plastic manufacturers, and let his innate talents do the job.

The example of Jim Stark can create the impression that every employee at CWC was recombinable and that I am claiming that there always exists an alternative to downsizing. Let's be clear: Such a claim would be grossly overselling the power of people recombination. Even at CWC, a firm replete with knowledgeable, skilled, well-networked, and innately talented employees, there were employees like Tom Green (a human resources manager), who spent most of his time reading the *Wall Street Journal* and did not add much value to the company.

Analyzing Green through the lens of the people recombinant framework indicated that he had some useful recombinants—primarily his wide-ranging network in the firm. But because of his "I couldn't give a hoot" demeanor, his staff had little respect for him, and in general Green was considered out of touch with the people at CWC. Still, Browning realized that Green's network would be hard to replicate and might prove to be extremely useful in selling the change to CWC employees. Moreover, the HR function would be critical during the division turnaround. Peter Browning decided, therefore, that before downsizing him, he would give Green a chance to meet a particular set of goals within a fixed time frame. In other words, he would give him a chance to recombine himself with the new CWC that Browning was trying to create.

In the final analysis, Green proved to lack characteristics at the bottom of the recombinant pyramid (values, aptitudes, and psychological traits, which are generally unlikely to change) that would make it possible to recombine him in the new CWC. So when Green was unable to make much change in his performance, Browning had no choice but to replace him (providing Green with a decent severance and out-placement package).

Finding People Recombinants

There is more than one way to go about asking the question "What people recombinants can I use in this situation?" At times, the way to pose the question imposes itself on decision makers. They face a clear and pressing problem—strategic or operational goals are clear, but they are not being achieved. Other times, decision makers face an unambiguous opportunity—they achieved their goal easily, and it is obvious that the goal was set too low and a lot more could be done. In both instances, the ends are crystal clear: Solve this problem or exploit that opportunity. The recombination question is even clearer: What people recombinants do I already control that could serve as means to the end of eliminating this problem or capitalizing on that opportunity? This, of course, is the means-to-ends recombination approach I described in chapter 2.

At other times, there is no clear strategic or operational goal driving the recombination effort initially. What is clear, instead, is that there exists some resource in the firm—a people recombinant, in the context of this chapter—that is extremely valuable but is either going unused or is underutilized. For example, the organization has a promising employee like Jim Stark whom it might have to downsize. What it doesn't know is how it could redeploy this employee. In other words, the leader or manager knows one or more employees who could be the means to a recombination, but she does not know to what end she can recombine this or these employees. The leader or manager faces a solution searching for a problem or an opportunity. The recombination question in these instances becomes: What problem or opportunity do I have that I could address using these people recombinants? This is the ends-for-means recombination approach.

People Means

The simplest way of using your people to create painless change is to begin with a particular end in mind—the change you want to foster— and then shop around the firm looking for existing recombinants in your employees that could be used. This sounds simple, but many firms miss such opportunities. Fortunately, we can learn from organizations such as the U.S. Army, which is quite skillful when it comes to redeploying people to solve a problem or to capitalize on a particular opportunity.

Such was the case with my brother, who made a career in the military. Like me, my brother is American but was brought up in France by American parents. Like me, he speaks English and French like a native speaker, but unlike me, he has a tremendous linguistic aptitude. He also speaks four other languages, including fluent Japanese—one of the three most difficult languages for a native English speaker to learn (the others are Arabic and Korean). It so happens that the U.S. Army is always in need of Foreign Area Intelligence Officers (FAIOs) who are familiar with foreign cultures and can speak their languages—particularly if they speak Japanese, Arabic, or Korean.

Yet when my brother joined the army after earning a college degree in East Asian studies and living for two years in Japan, the army did not choose to train him to become an FAIO. Instead, he joined the elite 82nd Airborne paratrooper division and rose to the rank of major. Rather than using his tremendous linguistic aptitudes, he was taught to jump out of planes at night with a 150-pound rucksack and to parachute into enemy positions, where he had to defend himself by every means and to lay out landing fields for the main wave of paratroopers. He probably would have ended his career as a top-ranking officer in the 82nd Airborne had he not decided to recombine himself into an army intelligence position in order to exploit his linguistic abilities.

How, you might wonder, does this story demonstrate the U.S. Army's proficiency at recombining the skills and knowledge of its people toward new ends? Certainly, on the surface, this appears to be yet another example of a large and wasteful governmental bureaucracy that is incapable of spotting and recombining the precious individual assets it already commands. Indeed, why did not the army detect my brother's tremendous linguistic aptitudes when it recruited him? Or if it did, why did it not immediately put him in an FAIO job that fully exploited this precious recombinant? What a blunder!

What such reasoning misses is that had the army placed my brother at an FAIO desk job when they recruited him, he would have simply quit. Why? Because my brother joined in order to "be all that he could be" in extreme battle-front conditions, in order to defend his country. He did not join to sit at some desk deep in the bowels of the Pentagon, in an office rendered windowless for security reasons. The key recombinant the army could employ when my brother became an officer was his deeply patriotic individual values, his athletic aptitudes, and his psychological need for an extreme physical and martial challenge. More generally, in the all-volunteer U.S. Army, where the financial incentives are often well below those that a highly educated and skilled volunteer could earn in the business sector, the key recombinant that the army has to draw upon is the volunteer's patriotic values and psychological drive.

By the same token, the army has to make it possible for its volunteers to find career paths that simultaneously capitalize on their values and psychological drives and that use their unique aptitudes, knowledge, and skills. After years of special-forces-type operations, my brother was ready to exploit his unique linguistic abilities in the context of a more "peaceful" army career. At that point, the army had the systems in place to make it possible for my brother to recombine himself. In other words, what the army knows is that recombining an employee to solve a problem or exploit an opportunity is not always something that superiors do to subordinates. It can be extremely effective to have systems in place for subordinates to decide voluntarily to recombine themselves to solve their superiors' problems or exploit their opportunities.

I tell my brother's case with the focus on one individual, with one idiosyncratic set of recombinants. It provides a good illustration of how to recombine one individual to make small-scale change in an organization, effectively recombining your way to less painful change. Moreover, it begins to suggest how an institution might structure itself to recombine not just one volunteer, like my brother, but many such volunteers in order to pull off a large-scale recombination. What the example does not do, however, is illustrate the process by which leaders who notice a group of employees with unique recombinants go about posing the question: What particular ends could these employees be the means to?

Ends for People

When the German railroad company Deutsche Bahn faced an environment in which railroads had reached a saturation point, the company lost the need for a large planning and project function for building new railroads. One option would have been to eliminate the planning and project department and to lay off its entire staff. Deutsche Bahn, however, adopted another technique that it has reused repeatedly ever since: It considered how it might recombine its staff of skilled planners and project managers to a new end.

The answer was to spin off the planning department as an independent company. This new company allowed Deutsche Bahn to continue using these employees when it needed them for planning and project functions, but to keep them employed by having them in a self-sustaining company that could serve customers other than Deutsche Bahn. Now well established, this company employs many people, all of whom would have lost their jobs had the railroad chosen a more creatively destructive and painful approach. Deutsche Bahn, then, effectively recombined employees by pulling together an entirely new company using existing human resources.

Great recombiners have more than one trick in their bag when it comes to finding recombinants. They also have a full bag of tricks when it comes to techniques for actually using these recombinants painlessly and effectively. I turn to these next.

How to Recombine

Chapter 2 described three techniques for using creative recombination to create change without pain: cloning, customizing, and translating. As you will recall, each technique requires not only different types of implementation processes, but also different types of supporting knowledge in order to implement it properly.

When it comes to recombining aspects of your people, using the right technique for each type of recombinant—and supporting it with the right resources—will mean the difference between making a successful change or not. In general, recombinants on the bottom level of the pyramid-shaped people recombinant framework introduced earlier in this chapter—values, aptitudes, and psychology—aren't easily changeable and are therefore very difficult to either clone, customize, or translate. People characteristics found in the middle of the pyramid—namely, demeanor and networks—can be customized or translated to fit a new situation, but rarely cloned (as I'll explain in more detail later in this section). With the topmost level of recombinants—knowledge and skills—you can pretty much use any of the three techniques, depending on the situation, and it should work.

Cloning People Recombinants

Tom Green at CWC lacked certain values and aptitudes that would have made it possible to recombine him. Here is where cloning comes in: Browning replaced Green with a woman who was at the time an HR employee at Bondware, the Continental Can company Browning had just downsized. She had all the recombinants that were needed for the HR position at CWC—everything on the pyramid framework, including not only the right knowledge and skills but also the network and demeanor as well as the values, aptitudes, and psychology that Green lacked. She was a perfect fit. Browning was able to almost literally pick her up from Bondware and drop her into Green's job at CWC, where she performed admirably and helped move the division to make the kinds of shifts in staff that would help it become more market driven and productive. In effect, Browning "cloned" her recombinants by moving her from one environment to another.

This brings up an important point. Although many people recombinants found in the pyramid framework can in fact be cloned to create positive changes in an organization, whole individuals, of course, cannot be cloned (yet). Fortunately, people come as a whole package of recombinants. They comprise a range of knowledge and skills, demeanors and networks, and values, aptitudes, and psychological traits. As we saw in the case of Stark, several of those recombinants (such as knowledge and skills) can in fact be easily cloned to create positive changes in an organization, without having to look outside the firm for all new people. (Although, unfortunately, that wasn't the case with Tom Green.) Only in rare cases will individuals—such as the woman that Peter Browning brought into CWC from a sister company—have the exactly right bundle of recombinants to clone seamlessly into a new situation, that is, all the necessary knowledge, skills, demeanor, networks, values, aptitudes, and psychology to function effectively in that situation.

Customizing People Recombinants

A quick glance at the pyramid framework tells us how easy or hard it will be to develop or otherwise change particular people recombinants. It makes it possible to decide, therefore, whether a manager should redeploy a person in order to effect a specific change—and, if so, how much customization this will require.

Most employees have many more characteristics (e.g., knowledge of a particular topic, skills to carry out a special task) than those for which they were hired or which they use in their job. So, to provide ample opportunity for recombination, a good place to begin is by taking inventory of these unused skills. Unlike characteristics toward the bottom of the pyramid, you can relatively easily train employees in knowledge and skills that they lack—as was the case with Stark's knowledge of plastic closures.

This relative ease in training for knowledge and skills underlies the maxim used in many highly successful firms to "hire for attitude and train for skills." Southwest Airlines, for instance, tends to hire flight attendants with backgrounds in teaching and social work rather than the airline industry. They assume that customer-centric values are absolutely necessary to excel at Southwest and are extremely hard to develop in new hires. Skills, such as handing out peanuts, are not.

A second approach—job rotation—does not rely on formal training to customize an employee's knowledge and skill set to fit into a particular job or position. So-called stretch assignments are assignments in which an employee possesses enough of the skills and knowledge necessary to function in the job to which he or she is recombined, but not all the skills and knowledge needed to excel in that job. Rotating employees into such stretch assignments causes them to learn, on the job, the remaining knowledge and skill they need to excel in those jobs. Such learning-by-doing can be very valuable for a firm that recombines its employees rather than downsizing them. Indeed, as its employees move from stretch assignment to stretch assignment, they not only learn an increasing variety of knowledge and skills but also learn how to learn, making them increasingly redeployable and recombinable.

Much more difficult to customize and recombine are people who lack the recombinants appearing on the second level of our pyramid framework: demeanor and networks. Usually, coaching or counseling offers a longer-term solution. Hardest to recombine are people who lack recombinants at the bottom level of the pyramid. As you will recall, the problem with Tom Green, the HR manager at CWC, ultimately had to do with his values, aptitudes, and psychological traits. Having worked in the division for decades, Green simply lacked the motivation he would need to help retrain (or recruit) and manage a staff that would push the division to new levels of success. He ultimately had to be replaced with someone who would.

In short, there are certain blocks that simply won't fit into certain holes: You cannot turn Green into something that he, in his very essence, is not. On the flip side, I see many firms miss tremendous opportunities to customize by redeploying their employees, that is, putting employees with a mix of customizable characteristics (top of the pyramid) and noncustomizable characteristics (bottom of the pyramid) into positions or teams that need people with those characteristics. Most recently, for instance, I watched a California software firm that failed to realize that Hispanics would made up a rapidly increasing percentage of its customer base. Indeed, by 2025, an estimated 17 percent of all U.S. citizens will be of Hispanic origin,[6] and the percentage in California will be much higher. Yet this firm completely missed the opportunity to leverage the values, skills, and sensitivities of its Hispanic employees to gauge access and develop markets for its software. This firm is blind to a rich source of people recombinants who are increasingly growing in importance, with valuable inputs that include aesthetic sensitivities such as taste as well as an understanding of the preferences of a particular ethnic, regional, or socioeconomic group.

Translating People Recombinants

Like customizing, translating becomes increasingly difficult to use as we work our way down the pyramid. As a rule, translating has very limited uses when it comes to recombinants at the bottom of the pyramid (values, aptitudes, and traits). Every rule has an exception that confirms it, however. Returning to our example of CWC, Peter Browning was able to translate one of these lower-level recombinants. Let's look at how.

Browning crafted one final change in the division through a key individual: Bob White, the son of the division's founder. Although at the time that Browning came on the scene Bob White had recently retired, he still remained a looming figure in the culture of Continental White Cap. He possessed two extremely valuable recombinants. The first was the broad-ranging network of people he knew in the division and who, more important, knew and trusted him. In the primarily paternalistic culture of CWC, Bob White was the "Dad" and the division's employees were his "children." The second recombinant was White's personal values, which were the same ones he and his father before him had imprinted on the firm: loyalty, hard work, and inventiveness.

Peter Browning saw both of those recombinants as things that he could leverage to create the changes needed in the division. The first recombinant, White's network, was easily recombinable to the new kind of market-driven division that Browning was charged with crafting. Once Browning was able to meet with White and get him on board with the proposed changes, White was able to deliver that message to his entire network within CWC.

The second recombinant, White's values, would be impossible to change within White himself. He would always stand for the values that he had developed for decades in the business. Was it possible, however, to translate these "White values" for employees so that the values were more suited to the competitive challenge that CWC was facing? That was one question that Browning wanted to at least attempt to answer. More specifically, White embodied the value of innovativeness—but not of market-driven innovativeness. Browning had to translate for a new context what White stood for. White also embodied the values of company paternalism and employee loyalty to the paternalistic company. That loyalty, however, seemed to be aimed more toward White directly rather than toward the broader goal of a successful division. So the task was not to transform White; it was to translate the values that White represented in a way that stressed that being loyal to the firm meant helping it perform effectively.

What this final part of the CWC example illustrates is that although it might not be possible to change the values, aptitude, or psychology of a person, when that individual stands as a symbol in a corporate culture, it may be possible to translate the meaning of that symbol in order to recombine it with new business conditions. We will return to this use of symbolic recombinants in chapter 5, which pertains to recombining corporate culture. Before doing so, however, chapter 4 takes a more in-depth look at the challenge of recombining informal social networks.

From Ideas to Practice

This section of the chapter, like that of subsequent chapters, addresses "when" and "where" questions. It aims to bridge the divide between ideas about tools and the art and practice of using them to get results. It does so by providing guidelines for when the mapping, search, and action techniques presented earlier are appropriate. It also provides examples of how corporation leaders and managers are putting these techniques to use today.

Complex recombinants, such as people, create a very large (almost infinite) array of recombinatory possibilities. This section can outline only some of the many examples of how companies recombine people. Others can be found at the Web site ChangeWithoutPain.com as readers of this book post them there.

The previous section examined in detail how a change leader (Peter Browning) redeployed and recombined people using the tools of cloning (Green), customizing (Stark), and translating (White). This example probably brought to mind how you—as a change leader or manager—use these tools, and how you might put them to even greater use. Because I have discussed in detail the application of the action tools of cloning, customizing, and translating to individuals, this section focuses on how to apply such tools to larger numbers of people.

Recall the very different type of example I provided of my brother, an army major who, on his own initiative, redeployed and recombined his extensive linguistic skills by making the change from being an elite paratrooper to becoming a Foreign Area Intelligence Officer. This example raises the following question: What existing properties of your firm and employees can you leverage to encourage employees to redeploy and recombine themselves for their own good and that of the firm? I examine first the techniques and tools, like so-called e-cruiting, that facilitate the self-recombination of employees.

You cannot, of course, recombine everyone. Leaders have to lay off employees—sometimes many employees. Certain companies, however, have turned this challenge into an opportunity. I provide examples of such techniques after examining self-recombination techniques like e-cruiting.

E-cruiting

We all remember how we used to encourage employees to recombine themselves with new jobs in the firm—via job opening announcements pinned on the bulletin board in the hall outside the personnel office. A rapidly growing number of firms have created in-house job boards by recombining the personnel office's bulletin board with the firm's Web page. Ideally, employees find self-recombination opportunities in their firm with one click of their mouse. This type of self-recombination comes naturally to employees who got their job at the firm from one of the many external job boards—whether an all-purpose job board such as Yahoo!'s Hotjobs.com or specialized job boards such as 6figures.com, which targets the job seeker looking for big bucks.

In short, smart companies have capitalized on the so-called e-cruitment trend through job boards to enable their employees to recombine themselves with new jobs in their firms that better serve the employees' needs as well as the company's needs. A group of 32 companies that includes Intel, Mutual of Omaha, Lockheed Martin, and IBM has taken this logic of recombination one step further: They have recombined their in-house job boards to create DirectEmployers.com, the mother of all self-recombination search engines.

Job boards, like many other Web-based knowledge retrieval technological fixes, have their downside, however. The information available about people's recombinants is sketchy, even when the more sophisticated search tools are used. A lot of self-recombination (40 percent, according to Forrester Research)[7] still occurs through good old-fashioned social networks, which provide the rich information about whether an individual has the skills, knowledge, network, demeanor, values, aptitudes, and personality necessary to be redeployed from one part of the firm to another. Smart firms know how to leverage these existing networks. Intel, for example, reports that half of its hires come not from job boards but from its employee referral program.

Alumni Networks

Consider the example of Audrey, a knowledgeable, skilled, and well-networked real estate attorney working at Brown & Wood, the New

York–based corporate law firm. As the firm faced mounting financial turmoil, rather than lay off Audrey outright, Joan, her supervising attorney, gave in to Audrey's long-standing request to work part-time. This could not save her job, however, and a few months before Brown & Wood was acquired by another firm, Joan laid off Audrey, to everyone's consternation.

Although Joan had severed the employment relation, she did not sever the network relation—she invited Audrey to parties, receptions, and even corporate events. During this period, Audrey landed a top job in a city agency regulating the real estate industry. Then, the real estate market reignited in the 1990s, creating a sellers' market for attorneys like Audrey—particularly those with high-level government experience and networks. Joan offered to rehire Audrey, and she accepted a part-time job at double her government salary. Contrast the case of Audrey with that of Joan, which was presented in chapter 1. The latter would probably rather die than ever rejoin Cisco, however sweet the offer.

Contrast also Cisco to another Palo Alto firm—Agilent Technology, a diversified technology company in the communications, electronics, and life sciences industries. When Agilent had to lay off eight thousand employees, it created an alumni network of ex-Agilent employees in the hope of rehiring them when conditions improved. Agilent had revived an old idea—Bain, the consulting firm, formed an alumni network seventeen years ago. This highly active network of over four thousand ex-Bain employees has become not only a source of rehires—employees who are well acquainted with its culture and practices and who can easily be recombined into consulting assignments—but also a source of referral for new employees and business.

Retiring at Work

Volkswagen provides still another type of example. In the late 1980s and early 1990s, it decided to redeploy and recombine its retirees. The company's retirement scheme had engendered a huge cost-structure problem at Volkswagen because the high retirement payment to retirees, characteristic of German industry, was multiplied by the large number of retirees. The executives knew they needed to find something to do with these aging but still productive employees. Volkswagen was sitting on a powerful recombinant—the skills, experience, and knowledge of a segment of its people—if it could only figure out what end it could serve.

When the Volkswagen executives framed the ends-for-means question in these terms, the answer presented itself easily and clearly: Why not use these older Volkswagen employees to mentor and coach new assembly line workers? Who else was more highly skilled, experienced, and attuned to Volkswagen's cultural values and norms? Who else could better help new recruits cope with the complexity, stresses, and exhaustion of the modern assembly line? Not only would the mentor's protégées benefit, but so would the mentors, who would now have something highly meaningful to work for as they approached the end of their careers—namely, mentoring the next generation of Volkswagen employees. Volkswagen made the bold step, especially for a German firm, of placing assembly line workers over age 57 on part-time assignment for two years, at 75 percent of their current salary, if they agreed to serve as mentors.

Turning Downsizing into a Business

Not to be outsmarted by the likes of Bain and Volkswagen, other companies forced to downsize have extended the recombinatory logic one step further. I already mentioned in this chapter the example of Deutsche Bahn, which, rather than downsizing part of its operation, spun it off, retaining the option to hire ex-employees' services from the self-sustaining spin-off as needed. I also mentioned, in chapter 1, GKN's even more ingenious approach. Rather than downsizing engineers made redundant by contract cancellations, it created a business, GKN Engage, that rented out these engineers. In other words, it used its reputation for attracting topflight engineers, as well as its talent for developing engineering skills and its extensive network of contacts, to start what was, for all intents and purposes, a highly-sophisticated employment agency.

When to Recombine People

The book's introduction argued forcefully that prescriptions for action without qualifiers of when you should use them create the impression that they work everywhere, in many ways that suit your idiosyncratic needs, and with guaranteed superior results—promises that can never be fulfilled and that invariably lead to disappointment with the prescribed technique. Therefore, what guidelines are useful in addressing the "when to recombine people" question?

First and foremost, people recombination has to be equally or more effective and efficient, in both financial and human terms, than alternative options such as creative destruction, whether by small-scale layoffs and rehiring or by large-scale, strategic downsizing. Chapters 1 and 2 made the case that change avoiders can benefit most from creative destruction. Creative recombination, to the contrary, best fits changeaholics—firms that have changed like crazy and suffer, or are about to suffer, from acute repetitive-change syndrome. This is particularly true when it comes to creatively recombining people.

Reconsider the Cisco example from chapter 1. Until the end of 2000, Cisco pursued an extremely rapid expansion strategy, acquiring companies left and right and adding an average of 1,000 employees a month. The downturn in the telecom sector hit Cisco's performance hard; its all-out growth strategy had already given it a bad case of repetitive-change syndrome. By 2001, John Chambers, a leader who had built Cisco on the promise of empowerment and no layoffs, had to reverse course and order the first of what was to be four successive waves of downsizing. Repetitive-change syndrome, already bad in the upswing phase, became worse in the downswing.

With 20-20 hindsight, we all can see that less hiring and firing would have saved Cisco tremendous growth and downsizing pain. In particular, Cisco and firms like it teach us two clear lessons. First, little adds more quickly to initiative overload and the change-related chaos of a growth phase than the added work for existing employees of adding new employees. Listen again to Joan: "Cisco management was blind to the tremendous costs of hiring and reorganizing for growth— teams had to be redone, work assignments had to be redone, everything had to be relearned and, for a couple of months, nothing got done because everybody had to figure what to do." Second, little adds more to repetitive-change syndrome's cynicism and burnout than watching close work acquaintances be fired—particularly when a no-layoff vow is broken, as it was at Cisco, and when fewer people are left to do the same amount of work.

Even when repetitive-change syndrome mandates creative recombination, it requires people who have something to recombine. The employees of changeaholic firms often have these recombinants. The many, varied changes they have made provide them with a wealth of knowledge, skills, and networks that they can redeploy and recombine to reach new ends. This is not true for the employees of change-averse firms, particularly if the firm underinvested in developing its work force or overinvested in hiring and developing narrow specialists—people who know more and more about less and less until they know virtually everything about virtually nothing. Such specialists become so fitted to one job or situation that they become virtually unrecombinable with almost any other.

This book provides mapping, searching, and action tools for redeploying and recombining employees. Moreover, such tools already exist in many firms. To be useful, however, leaders and managers have to use these tools. Key to attempting change by recombination is the willingness, encouragement, and opportunity for employees and managers alike to use such tools. I return to this idea throughout the book, but particularly in the final chapter.

From Recombining Individuals to Recombining Their Social Networks

Returning to the Peter Browning case, it is interesting to note that in his previous position, he had to turn around another division of Continental Can, namely, Bondware. Without going into the details of this case, it suffices to say that Bondware was a true change-averse firm—a firm on the verge of extinction that contained almost no recombinants to reuse and redeploy. Browning the creative recombiner therefore had to become Browning the creative destroyer. In this instance, creative destruction was the road to change with the least amount of pain.

The brilliance of a leader like Browning is that he is not a one-trick turnaround artist—a kind of hatchet man brought in to butcher a firm in the hope that it will survive. When he arrived at CWC, he realized that the path to change with minimal pain was creative recombination, not creative destruction. He saw that CWC was a rich trove of people recombinants. He also saw (as we will when I return to the CWC example in subsequent chapters) that the firm's culture contained many other types of recombinants that he could revive, redeploy, and recombine.

This chapter stressed the importance of an individual's networks as a recombinant. Individuals, however, always network with other individuals, giving birth to large social networks that span hundreds, thousands, millions, and even billions of individuals. Most people by now are familiar with the six degrees of separation thesis. The people you know are one degree of separation away from you. The people these people know are two degrees, and the people these people know are, in turn, three degrees away from you. Travel six degrees of separation in your network, and you will find that Joe knows Bill, who knows Swen, who knows Abule, who knows Mombasa, who, in turns, knows Nelson Mandela.

In the next chapter, I turn to these vast social networks and to how firms can recombine small parts, or even large parts, of the networks that span not only the firm but also its suppliers, customers, regulators, and even its competitors.

4 Leveraging Social Networks Rather Than IT Networks

ELOITTE TOUCHE TOHMATSU *(DTT) is a global organization with revenues of over $13 billion, generated in 140 countries. Historically, like most large accounting firms, DTT was the product of a long series of mergers and acquisitions of practices, which had left the firm a little fragmented. Offices around the world needed better coordination if the firm hoped to continue attracting large, global clients. The senior partners knew that the firm had to globalize more swiftly and efficiently. Specifically, it needed to provide a homogenous, tightly coordinated level of service across many countries to its big clients. But how to go about making such a radical change?*

One way would be to creatively destroy the current structure of the organization and its various offices worldwide, whose leaders had been put in place as a result of their professional—rather than managerial—expertise. In effect, these professionals had been running their offices as semiautonomous local practices. Therefore, one option would be for the firm to reinvent itself by creating a new, global structure with new kinds of people—managers rather than professionals—overseeing work in regional divisions. In other words, it could move from a kind of federation of professional services firms to one large, coordinated corporation. Another approach would be to implement a massive IT knowledge-sharing network, which would make it possible for partners in every practice across the world to share all forms of information, support, and connections.

DTT has relied on some IT and some restructuring to achieve its highly successful globalization effort. But having watched companies in other industries attempt such changes— and seeing the kind of widespread pain that usually resulted from the firings and general chaos (not to mention extra costs) that attended such radical change—DTT chose another primary option. It has become a more globally connected company by capitalizing on the social networks of the partners it already had in place. In the end, DTT achieved the goal of coordinating its offices worldwide at much lower costs to the organization. By its actions, it would teach me an unforgettable lesson about how to approximate the ideals of change without pain.

This chapter examines in depth one type of recombinant introduced in chapter 2: networks. It focuses not only on *individual networks* (i.e., the networks of single individuals) but also on the recombinants offered by the networks that interlink many individuals in a firm. These latter networks are *social networks* that an organization's leaders can learn to reuse, redeploy, and recombine to bring about change with less pain. Let us begin with a look at what exactly leaders can recombine within and across networks.

What to Recombine

An examination of the recombinants found in organizational networks should probably begin with a picture of what those networks look like. Figure 4-1 offers a good map of what the network system at an organization such as DTT might look like.

FIGURE 4 - 1

Network Map

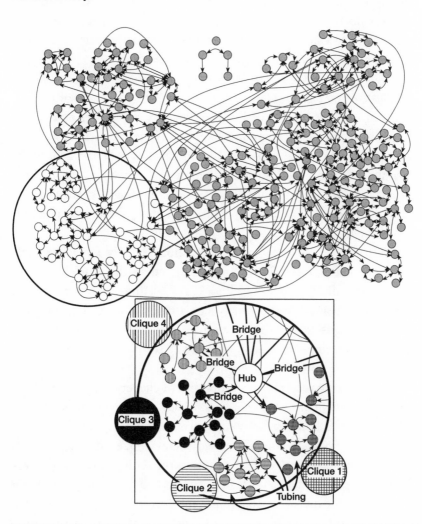

The intricacy of the figure alone should give you an indication of just how extensive and far-reaching networks can be and of the power to create change that this ability to connect people implies. Let's look at what elements you can recombine in such a firmwide network, using the specifics of this diagram as an illustration.

The Network Recombinant Framework

Several elements of networks can be found in the corporate basement and recombined in varying degrees to foster change. Although they don't fit neatly into a hierarchical pyramid like the people recombinants did, we can think of these network recombinants as clusters, cliques, bridges, hubs, and organizational plumbing.

Clusters and Cliques   Note in figure 4-1 that some areas of the networks are dense thickets of linkages, such as the cluster of contacts depicted in the figure's circular blowup. These clusters may mirror structural boundaries, such as the boundaries of a department. They may also mirror more informal groupings—the network of smokers, for instance, who meet regularly outside the building to share a puff, or the global network of people who share ideas about global supply chain management.

Clusters contain even smaller and more densely networked sub-clusters called *cliques*. The cluster depicted in the figure's circular blowup contains four distinct cliques. These cliques may form among small work teams, or they may constitute informal categories: a group of people who go to lunch every day and trade work-related gossip, for instance, or a group belonging to one small ethnic group in the firm.

What are the recombinant properties of clusters and cliques? Consider the example of smoker networks. They meet regularly outside the entrance to the building, in compliance with local regulations. They talk as they smoke, and often form very dense cliques. In large firms, or if there are many smokers, they can form entire network clusters. These smoker cliques and clusters cut across different parts of the firm—different divisions, functions, and locations. The smoker clusters and cliques also cross-cut different hierarchical categories of employees, ranging from the very junior to the very senior. They may even range outside the firm to different types of stakeholders and constituents—customers, regulators, and suppliers—who visit the firm regularly.

Jokingly, I tell people in seminars that they should not smoke, but rather pretend to smoke in order to gain access to the broad, cohesive, and wide-ranging smoker networks both at their firm and at those of their customers. Indeed, because of their wide-ranging nature, these networks are excellent sources of all forms of ideas, information, and knowledge about recombinants.

Clusters and cliques not only circulate recombinants, but are themselves recombinant. For the most part, networks emerge naturally, serendipitously, and informally. Frequently, networks emerge because the formal structure of the firm does not provide the supports necessary to carry out work. You can then leverage these spontaneously emerging networks to solve the problem that engendered their existence.

Consider the case of Columbia Business School, which has always been on the cutting edge of technological developments supporting education and was a very early adopter of computers. Like many early adopters of this technology, the leaders of the school did not fully foresee the technical complexity, problems, and opportunities that it would create. It therefore lagged in creating an IT support department. As a result, an informal network of faculty, administrators, and even students emerged spontaneously to swap all forms of IT information, hardware, software, patches, tips, and tricks to use and exploit computer technology. Call this network element the "computer geek clique."

What did the geek clique enable? The geeks were a temporary solution to a problem that grew with the number of users and the complexity of technology. In time, a clone of the excellent IT support system that functioned at the level of the entire university was recombined with the small business-school IT staff, as well as some university IT people. One major problem remained, however—a problem that most computer users who have "interfaced" with an IT support specialist have experienced. The gap in technological lingo and know-how between IT specialists and users produced a connection full of mutual condescension, hostility, and misunderstanding.

What could be done? Very simply, rename the geek clique the "Faculty Computing Committee" and have it meet regularly with the head of the IT department in order to bridge the divide between IT users and support staff. The Faculty Computing Committee at Columbia Business School survives to this day and has become a key ingredient of the outstanding computer service at the school. It is a living example of how it is possible to take a network clique, formalize it, and recombine it with existing processes to enable painless change.

Bridges and Hubs As the blowup in figure 4-1 indicates, networks contain *hubs*. Hubs have network relations with cliques and clusters that would be otherwise unconnected in networks. In the particular example in figure 4-1, the hub serves as a network *bridge* between the four cliques in the cluster. Without this hub, the cliques would be almost completely disconnected and incapable of sharing information with each other.

Consider another real-life example: the classic case of John Clendenin at Xerox. This case is used extensively to illustrate how networks function in organization. The case, however, also teaches us a very different and important lesson that is hardly mentioned in the instructions for using the case:[1] namely, that certain people, who occupy hub positions in social networks, can be invaluable to organizations. The bridging functions they serve—providing a communication flow that spans clusters and cliques—can be redeployed and recombined to bring about change throughout an organization. Xerox, in this case, saw in John Clendenin's network a rich means that could be redeployed and recombined repeatedly to the end of creating a communication bridge between the four main divisions of Xerox.

Xerox first hired John Clendenin, an ex-army officer, as a summer intern between his first and second year at Harvard Business School. Over the summer, Clendenin tinkered with two projects: one that eliminated overpackaging to the tune of $300,000 a year, and another that cut out a supply chain link that meant a $2 million savings for Xerox. It turned out that Clendenin was a master recombiner who plied his trade with stunning success. His summer successes were only a preamble of things to come.

Impressed by Clendenin's exploits, USMG (the regional division of Xerox in the United States) hired him as an internal consultant in the parts and supply department; within a year, it promoted him to department manager. Here is where Clendenin's story turns into a story of an ends-for-means recombination in which an organization used one individual's network to find problems it could solve. In his new position, Clendenin began by building a strong alliance with a Xerox old-timer, Tom Gunnings. Gunnings possessed a broad network crisscrossing many Xerox divisions. As a result, Clendenin's network now was a clone of Gunnings's, spanning multiple levels of the Xerox hierarchy as well as all four of its regional businesses—not only USMG in the United States, but also Fuji Xerox in Japan, Rank Xerox in Europe, and American Operations in South America.

Clendenin became a hub—an individual who has the informal network to see the whole of an organization and to exploit synchronizing and recombining opportunities. His network in place, Clendenin made an interesting career move. He lobbied people in the upper reaches of his network for a job shift to a miniscule unit, the Multinational Development Center (MDC), staffed by five employees with a $400,000 budget. Two years later the unit had a $4 million budget. Moreover, Clendenin staffed MDC with 42 employees.

What happened? Clendenin's wide-ranging network allowed him to see that MDC sat at the very center of the Xerox network. It is one of the very few units that link Xerox's four regional divisions. Clendenin the recombiner saw an opportunity. Clendenin's MDC can serve two key functions for Xerox. One is arbitrage. Indeed, Clendenin has found out, through his network, that the same copier parts can have four very different names across Xerox's four regional businesses. As a result, a part can clog up Fuji's inventory and be in extremely short supply at Rank. Because the parts have different names, however, Rank cannot recognize that it could obtain Fuji's surplus. Clendenin is the only network link synchronizing these different parts of Xerox and capable of moving excess inventory from one Xerox division to another.

MDC also delivers cheap recombinations to executives in Xerox's four internal divisions. For example, Clendenin discovered that the businesses were programming in the outdated COBOL programming language. He drew on some of his employees' existing expertise in C programming and delivered computer solutions at half the price. Because Clendenin's network spans the four major divisions of Xerox, he can distribute his solutions throughout the firm.

Organizational Plumbing Networks contain one final recombinant capability: They act as the organization's plumbing system. Each line linking two people in figure 4-1 is a section of social plumbing. Through this plumbing flows varied types of information and support vital to leveraging and recombining a firm's existing strengths. Moreover, this organizational plumbing system carries not only information but also mutual support. This support can be the political backing, the funding, or even the friendship that helps navigate a recombination toward successful, painless change.

What are the properties of organizational plumbing? Think of fiber optics. Fiber optic cable providers now thread their cables through obsolete tubing that once carried gas to buildings in busy downtown areas for gas lighting. Reusing these channels costs a fraction of what putting down new channels would have, assuming that busy downtown areas would ever have allowed the disruption caused by such infrastructural construction.

Likewise, you can recombine any piece of social network plumbing in your firm to transmit a different type of information or support than it did previously. For instance, I have often seen executives use the gossip network as a means of circulating information at lightning speed throughout the organization. That is precisely what the leadership team at DTT did when it redeployed what was naturally channeled through its internal plumbing—things such as favor exchanges, gossip, friendship, and information of all kinds—to help various parts of the firm coordinate better at the global level.

Of course, it is one thing to understand conceptually what parts of your firm's networks you can recombine to create change. It's quite another to find useful network recombinants—a topic we will turn to now.

Finding Network Recombinants

Increasingly, firms are looking for way to redeploy and recombine specialized expertise across firms. In my experience, and as the vignette about DTT that introduced this chapter illustrates, many of these firms have grown disillusioned with information technology solutions to this opportunity. They have put in the big computer networks, painfully collected, classified, and categorized expertise and placed it on these intranets, and beseeched their employees to not only draw from but also add to these expert systems. The systems fail because they do not work or they work too well. In the former case, the formal IT process exists, but no one uses it. In the latter case, everyone uses it and over time it becomes like the World Wide Web: There are diamonds of recombinant information in the rough, but one has to search through so much garbage to find them that it is hardly worth it.

Frequently, firms are trying to supplement or even replace IT solutions with face-to-face (or at least phone-to-phone) information exchange. These mechanisms take many names, perhaps the most popular being *knowledge teams, communities of practice,* and *caucuses.* Teams of knowledgeable employees meet to share and disseminate their particular brand of information and knowledge. This knowledge ranges from postmerger integration skills to how to survive as a woman or African American in the corporate world. Information shared can then be recombined within the team and across the firm as a whole.

I have watched many attempts to create these communities of practice. People start with the best intentions. However, unless there is a real return to each community member for taking the time in her busy work life to give and take from the community, enthusiasm dissipates rapidly.

A much easier technique is to take existing cliques or clusters that are already lying around the corporate basement—people who are already trading this information—and to formalize them. In other words, use an existing means for a brand-new end.

Network Means

The geek clique at Columbia Business School offers one example of taking an existing aspect of a network to create a new end—in this case the formal network called the Faculty Computing Committee. But consider too the growth of the civil rights, gay rights, and feminist movements. Many firms and employees have suffered the kind of explicit and implicit discrimination that keeps certain classes of employee from rising to the very top of corporate hierarchies.

Formal discrimination is relatively easy to address with formal organizing processes—standardizing promotion criteria, for instance. Informal discrimination, however, is much harder to abolish. One of its causes, research indicates, is not out and out discrimination. Rather, it results from *homopholy,* the tendency of people of similar backgrounds to network together, sometimes at the expense of people from other backgrounds.

Xerox is well known for its capacity to recombine materials and products. What is less well known is that it also has a tremendous track record in recombining informal organizational processes. Take, for example, the network cluster of African American employees that formed at Xerox as a result of the civil rights movement. Because of the difficulty they had accessing other Xerox networks (and the career-related information they circulated), Xerox's African American employees provided each other with informal career information and advice. Fortunately, Xerox had the foresight to encourage and formalize such networks (which it called caucuses) as a means of integrating other minorities into the firm's network. GE has similar caucuses that leverage the experience of employees from different ethnicities and backgrounds.

These examples illustrate the opportunity to leverage cliques and clusters—whether among minorities, smokers, or computer geeks—to reach particular ends. One simply needs to map the networks and leverage them, rather than attempt the more difficult, destabilizing, and painful process of starting from scratch.

Ends for Networks

You have a rich network, so what do you do with it? Networks can be solutions looking for a problem to solve or an opportunity to exploit. Returning to the Clendenin case, executives often have differing opinions about how to view Clendenin. Some cast Clendenin as the glorious hero in this situation, whereas others denigrate him as an evil empire builder. How dare he launch his own little profitable business within Xerox, even if it benefited Xerox? Why didn't Clendenin instead lead a restructuring of the global supply chain that would synchronize acquisition processes across the four Xerox businesses? Why did he not bring his programming ideas to the IT department and have them launch a C programming initiative across the firm?

Although at first the powers that be at Xerox also took this view, they soon came to see a potent means in their midst: Clendenin's networking abilities. And rather than discouraging the valuable ends that he produced (such as efficiently moving parts across regional divisions), Xerox chose to redeploy Clendenin for new ends by moving him yet again into another bridging position where he could reuse his network to accomplish similar feats.

So, instead of viewing Clendenin as a self-interested empire builder, Xerox saw him as someone who informally exploited tremendous recombination opportunities. It saw Clendenin's MDC as a wonderful mechanism that solved many problems that its senior managers did not even know existed. Xerox thus achieved efficient cross-germination across its four regional divisions without having to create something new. Because of Clendenin's network, no big, formal system needed to be put in place to conduct inventory management on a Xerox-wide basis. (Indeed, synchronizing the four divisions of an old, large, and successful organization might have taken decades.) Rather, change without pain prevailed. The next logical step would be for Xerox to institutionalize Clendenin's approach: to recombine this informal asset into a Xerox fixture and to grow it by cloning it—not to destroy it only to suffer through the difficult change process of recreating it.

Clendenin is a vital network hub, the model informal leader who empowers himself to solve business-wide problems smoothly and easily. He is the strategic networker who employs his large, wide-ranging set of contacts to discover such organization-wide problems and to recombine aggressively to solve them for the greater benefit of the firm. Many recombinants remain locked in Xerox's silos. A strategic networker such as Clendenin can bridge the structural chasms in Xerox's networks. He can carry across this bridge the precious seed of an idea locked in one silo, disseminate it to another, and use this knowledge in order to inseminate the next silo. Moreover, he verifies that this process runs effectively on an ongoing basis.

Clendenin's story illustrates both what an organization found (a person's network) to recombine in order to create painless change and how it framed the change as an ends-for-means solution. Once you have framed the issue of what aspects of your organizational networks you want to use to craft change, you are ready to decide what technique will foster the recombination most effectively.

How to Recombine

Recombining networks involves taking one network recombinant—a cluster, a clique, a bridge, a hub, or a section of organizational plumbing—and redeploying it for a new purpose. As we saw in chapter 3 in the case of people recombinants, you can clone, customize, or translate network recombinants to foster change.

Cloning Networks

Cloning a network recombinant means reusing the same cluster, clique, hub, bridge, or network tubing to create an opportunity or solve a problem. Generally, cloning a network involves one person reproducing another person's network exactly, by having the original networker introduce the new one to all of his or her network contacts and vouch for the new person's trustworthiness. This occurs frequently when one star salesperson allows a new salesperson to clone his network: The star introduces all his sales contacts to the younger person and vouches for that person's trustworthiness. This allows the star to move on and create new sales networks, which a new salesperson can then clone.

Another approach to cloning networks does not require literally reproducing the network by duplicating the contacts in another person's network. It may be sufficient just to bring that person and her network into a particular organizational clique or cluster.

Consider the case of Jerry Sanders, who with an investment of $180,000 founded X-Cardia—a company in the medical devices industry—which he sold in 1997 for $33 million to UroHealth, an established, fast-growing medical devices supplier.[2] How did he do it? A medical devices start-up, in its essence, is a recombination of four types of resources: investment capital, an idea for a medical device, a device prototype, and an established medical devices supplier willing to purchase the start-up. Sanders's network had the organizational plumbing through which the capital and ideas could flow to him. He had extensive contacts in the investment community, including private and so-called hook investors, who could reel in the financial backing of big institutional investors.

Sanders also had a strong network contact with Ascher Shmulewitz, a doctor certified in cardiology who had a Ph.D. in electrical and biomedical engineering. Dr. Shmulewitz is best described as a medical recombiner par excellence. His recombinations include recombining x-ray and ultrasound technology to detect early breast cancer—a recombination that Sanders helped him turn into a company called

NeoVision. Another recombination was the idea propelling X-Cardia. Shmulewitz took an idea that had existed since the 1930s—using electrical current and electrodes to measure blood resistance and cardiac output—and updated it by attaching these electrodes to the type of noninvasive tube that is already installed in many surgical heart patients. Presto, he had a noninvasive recombination for measuring cardiac output. It was nothing new—just some good old tinkering with medical stuff lying around the basement.

What Sanders lacked, however, to turn this medical device recombinant into a company was network tubing capable of channeling the other two other resources necessary for a medical device start-up: the prototype and the rich corporate customer looking to buy a prototype. One possibility would be to find someone with such a network and clone it by duplicating it. Even simpler would be to take such a person, give her a share of the start-up action, and add her network to the start-up clique you are forming. This is precisely what Sanders did when he brought Margaret McHenry, an executive with twenty years of experience in the medical industry, into the start-up. With her extensive network bridging both prototype manufacturers and well-established medical device suppliers shopping around for a hot idea, McHenry became just the network recombinant that Sanders needed—someone who could liaise with the prototype manufacturers in order to develop the X-Cardia prototype, and someone who could then sell the prototype to a medical devices supplier.

Customizing Networks

Unlike cloning, the manner in which network recombinants can be customized varies depending on whether you're customizing clusters and cliques, hubs and bridges, or organizational plumbing.

Customizing Clusters and Cliques An extensive body of research tells us that network plumbing is not like house plumbing.[3] Most network plumbing is highly redundant when it comes to carrying resources. Put differently, much—but by no means all—of a firm's network plumbing could be ripped out without affecting which resources flow around the firm.

Consider the rather extreme example of a division I'll call Island Engines, which makes turbines as part of a large global conglomerate.

When I first met its senior management team of thirteen executives, I was startled to notice that they all wore the same strange type of shoe—one they explained to me proudly was used exclusively on a particular type of sailing vessel unique to the island where they worked. In all fairness, however, their dress code did have two variants to go with the obligatory shoes: khaki pants with either a blue Oxford button-down shirt or a white Oxford button-down shirt.

Why this high level of similarity in their demeanors? By virtue of being collocated on an island, this team had lunch together every day in the executive cafeteria. Over time, they had introduced the other team members to their friends and contacts. As a result, each executive's network was a virtual clone of the others.

As an outsider listening to this tightly woven clique's conversations, it was clear that each executive tended to receive the same information again and again, sometimes as many as a dozen times, from the other executives. The plumbing interconnecting members of this clique and bridging their clique to other cliques was extremely redundant. As a result, not only did everyone in the clique know the same information, but they also interacted so often that they had the same view on life. Consequently, they tended to interpret the same information in the same way.

Tightly networked cliques have tremendous benefits: strong cohesion, extensive trust, and a powerful esprit de corps that will allow them to sail unscathed through the most difficult corporate storms. They also have tremendous liabilities, however, which must be considered when these teams are recombined: a redundancy of information and a narrowness of vision that does not characterize more diversely networked cliques and clusters.

Recombining such homogeneous cliques and clusters may therefore require some customization. It may be necessary to introduce some new, differently networked individuals in order to bring a greater diversity of information and perspectives to the clique or cluster. For example, helping the Island Engine executive team find, hire, and integrate into their team a few executives from outside their collective network could bring to the team the fresh information and perspectives that it drastically needed. It might also be necessary to coach the team in how to maintain the diversity the new executives would bring—and how not to turn them into three more Island Engineers.

Customizing Hubs and Bridges It is quite possible to recombine a network hub like Clendenin and the bridging function that he provided between the four disconnected businesses that constituted Xerox. Indeed, as I pointed out earlier, Xerox recombined Clendenin and his network twice, in other parts of Xerox, to utilize his bridging function.

Recombining network hubs, however, may often require some measure of customization. You will often have to add network tubing, or sever it, in order to fit hubs to another setting. This raises an even bigger customization challenge. Moreover, network tubing allows the greatest flow of resources when the people it connects trust each other. Indeed, in many firms people will not give up information, resources, or recombinants unless they can trust the recipient to keep certain types of precious information confidential or to reciprocate in time with his own recombinants. As was the case when Stark at CWC had to network with plastic container manufacturers, the key customization challenge in recombining a person who serves as a hub or a bridge is building that trust with new contacts added to his network.

Customizing Organizational Plumbing A firm's internal plumbing is the channel through which flows the know-why and know-when that is needed for accomplishing recombination through customization (see table 2-1). It is also the conduit for the know-what of the organization that's required for cloning, as well as the know-who and know-who-knows-who necessary to find out how to translate the means useful to reach an ends in one situation into similar means to the same ends in a very different situation.

Recombining what flows through a piece of network tubing can take different forms. One frequent approach is to recombine tubing carrying friendship flows with a business content. Citigroup, for instance, has been very successful in using the friendship flows of its employees to circulate insurance and financial planning products. Amway has done the same kind of thing with detergent, just as Tupperware has done with storage containers and Mary Kay has with cosmetics. In each of these examples, the friendship networks of employees become the tubing through which products and services can be transported and sold. Clearly, however, a friendship flow is very different from a product or service flow. The key, as illustrated by Mary Kay, is to train employees to turn buying cosmetics into a social experience.

You can customize network tubing by modifying not so much what flows through it but rather how what flows through it is utilized. The HR department at Microsoft, for instance, has been credited with keeping the firm together by leveraging informal gossip networks to find out which executives were unhappy or about to leave and then taking prompt action. A gossip flow, in other words, was customized to serve as an early warning information system. Clearly, such recombinations have to be customized with tremendous discretion and with the well-being of the firm at heart.

Translating Networks

Cloning and customizing involve reusing the same clusters, cliques, hubs, bridges, and tubing for either new or existing ends. Translating a network does not. Rather, it involves deciding how a particular network serves as the means to a particular end and then recreating a network of different people who serve the same end.

For example, after the success of X-Cardia, it was not difficult for Sanders to theorize about the ingredients for a successful start-up in the medical services industry. Namely, it needed a team of people with networks bridging into (1) the community of investors who provide start-up capital, (2) the community of scientists with the ideas for new medical devices, (3) the community of firms that produce prototypes of devices, and (4) the network of people in established medical devices suppliers. In the X-Cardia start-up, Sanders provided the bridge to community 1, Shmulewitz the bridge to community 2, and McHenry the bridge to communities 3 and 4. The question then becomes, Can someone translate this network formula for use in another industry, using a cast of characters other than our dynamic trio? Or can this trio translate this network formula to start up a business in another industry?

Consider another well-known example: Corning, the maker of specialty glasses, and its long history of cooperating with other firms through joint ventures and strategic alliances. Corning has a general formula for managing the network of relationships with joint venture partners and strategic allies. Trusting network linkages have to exist at the very top of the partnering firm—CEO to CEO. Corning executives responsible for sector strategies join the board of major new joint ventures to network with its members and then pass on the role to a group president. Network links must exist not only at senior levels, but also at every level of the joint venture partnership. This is only the template, of course. The actual network linking Corning to its joint venture partners has to be reinvented for every new major joint venture— but it is reinvented along this template.

From Ideas to Practice

Many and varied ways exist to help you put your social networks to work. I can only provide some suggestive examples in this section. They range from using your own personal network to leveraging your organization's network and to exploiting other organizations' networks. The key tool here is *social network analysis* (SNA), a series of techniques and programs to present social networks graphically. You can find out more about SNA at ChangeWithoutPain.com and even download network mapping tools.

When to Leverage Networks Using Social Network Analysis

SNA is based on an extensive body of academic research;[4] a bevy of easily available mapping tools exist, as well as many specialists in the use of these tools. They provide network maps like that depicted in figure 4-1. In such maps, the thickness of the lines marks the strength of network links, dotted lines indicate different types of relationships, and patterns indicate different types of people. A two-headed arrow denotes that a pair recognizes each other as network contacts, whereas a unidirectional arrow denotes a unidirectional relation. Working with the network contact maps on screen makes it possible to pull together different cliques and place a circle around them.

Such maps allow people to understand how their networks project themselves in the social world, and allow managers to understand how their subordinates' networks might be recombined and decombined. Once you have developed an accurate picture of your firmwide network, you're ready to determine where you might best find the kinds of clusters and cliques, hubs and bridges, and organizational plumbing that can be recombined. Before discussing the different ways SNA has been used, a qualifier is in order. Social network analysis is a powerful tool for exploiting network recombinants. Like many such tools, however, it is important to understand when it should be used and what are its limits. Otherwise, SNA promises to become a fad that will replace many failed knowledge management efforts.

The challenge in social network analysis is not so much the software to graph these networks, but rather to obtain high-quality data about network relationships that are graphed using the software. The challenge is minimal with personal networks or when the networks are small—circulating a questionnaire to people in the network makes it easy to obtain network data and to graph them. With larger networks, however, the task can be daunting. The key, then, is to leverage existing data. These data are becoming increasingly available: data about who e-mails whom in the firm, about who accesses which sites on the company Web page, about cell phone calls within the company, and so on, although these data raise privacy issues.

The broader question is whether SNA is a working or an educational tool. It is clearly useful for building sensitivity concerning how networks work and how you can leverage networks. My impression, however, is that when this sensitivity to networks has been developed by using SNA tools, skilled executives sense recombinant opportunities without having to graph entire networks every time.

These qualifiers out of the way, let's consider concrete examples of SNA in use. Companies develop expertise at managing change. IBM captures this change management expertise through its Transformation Unit and redeploys it to manage the next round of changes. Chip Drozenski, a senior Transformation Unit program manager, faced implementing the move to SAP software in IBM's vast fulfillment operation—a 30,000-employee logistics unit charged with shipping IBM products to 14 million customers globally. There was a lot at stake for Chip. I recently witnessed how one of these system changes in a large industrial services company produced a logistics catastrophe of such magnitude as to virtually destroy the firm's largest division.

Drozenski took an unusual step: mapping out the network of contacts between people involved in the change using a social network analysis program. What appeared was not a pretty picture. It revealed Drozenski embedded in a tightly knit network of senior managers—like those at Island Engine—who talked largely among each other. Very little network tubing carried information between this senior management clique and experts in the field. Moreover, the tubing that did exist carried a one-way information flow—from senior management to the field, not vice versa. Finally, large sections of network tubing that would be necessary to communicate with key stakeholders in the change effort did not exist. As a result, the senior management clique made implementation decisions with little input from the field, with the result that early phases of change efforts failed and had to be repeated.

Drozenski's network map was not all doom and gloom, however. The map revealed certain employees—network hubs—positioned in the social network to transmit vital change-related information, not only between the executive clique and the field but across different cliques and clusters throughout the field. Some of these hubs acted as information bottlenecks that needed to be unclogged; others served as information bridges that Drozenski could widen to get the two-way communication flow necessary to bring about change smoothly. In the end, Drozenski credited graphing and leveraging the social network with a "tenfold improvement in cross-functional communication."[5]

Putting Your Personal Network to Work

Drozenski's experience illustrates a simple lesson: You will have trouble leveraging and recombining your network if you cannot see what it looks like in its entirety. So give yourself half an hour and take a first, simple step. Graph your social network. Complex network graphing programs exist, but it is sufficient to depict your network on a large piece of paper (or download the simple Microsoft Excel–based network graphing tool at ChangeWithoutPain.com).

Using figure 4-1 as a model, enclose the names of your work-related contacts in circles and link these circles with arrows to depict not just your relationship to your contacts, but also the relationships among these contacts. Employ any other symbol that you find helpful to annotate the network graph, such as thicker lines to depict closer contacts, arrows for one-way contacts, or triangles to distinguish executives from people in the field. Spend some time graphing your contacts' key contacts—people you don't know personally, but who could be of great assistance if your contact introduced or contacted them for you. If you do not know for sure, a quick series of calls can help you fill out the network picture.

Now that you have a picture of your network, what do you know? Let's review a few key principles of networking. For the next few minutes, think of your social network purely as a tool that exists for the sole purpose of helping you carry out your work more efficiently and effectively—whether it be implementing SAP software, finding new customers, catching employee malfeasance, mentoring a subordinate, or finding out strategic information. Clearly, your network serves many other non-work-related functions, but put these aside for a while.

Focusing Your Network From this pragmatic perspective, bigger networks—in the sense of knowing more people—are not necessarily better. Executives' most precious asset often is time. Networking takes time, and maintaining bigger networks takes more time—time that is wasted if it provides little return on its investment. Consider, for example, Drozenski's tightly knit network of senior managers who talked largely only to each other. Each of Drozenski's contacts in the senior management group will bring him very little new information pertinent to the change because all these executives share pretty much the same information and the same perspective. In contrast, each additional network contact that creates a bridge from Drozenski to a network cluster in the field that is involved in the change brings in brand-new information interpreted from a very different field-level perspective. It also provides a back channel through which Drozenski can communicate to people in that network how to manage the change.

If there is one rule of networking, it is that in an optimized personal network, less is more: You should leverage a minimal number of contacts to maximize your work efficiency and effectiveness. Other nonessential contacts may provide benefits such as a sense of belonging, friendship, or juicy gossip. From a narrowly utilitarian perspective, however, the time invested in maintaining these network contacts does not provide sufficient work-related returns. Focusing your network by lessening how frequently you interact with nonessential contacts often provides the simplest way of better leveraging your personal network. It frees up time to exploit key contacts more fully and to employ this time to carry out other work-related activities.

Leveraging Key Contacts Another approach to leveraging personal networks involves better leveraging the key contacts in your network.

What makes a network contact a "key contact"? Obvious characteristics of useful contacts are factors such as their rank, reputation, expertise, and location in another unit of your firm or in a customer's firm—factors that determine whether this contact can help you do your job. Your map should highlight these types of contacts.

A second characteristic has to do with a network contact's willingness to help you. Can you trust this person to help you, even when it is not in her direct interest to do so? Will she take the time to give you the full and honest information, support, and knowledge that you require to do the best job possible? In other words, is this contact an ally—a person with whom you have a balanced relationship based on mutual help, support, and information sharing? At the extreme, can you count on this person to help you in a difficult situation, come hell or high water? Your network map should distinguish such close relationships from more distant ones.

The final characteristics of good contacts arise not from who they are, but from who they know. Particularly important, as Drozenski discovered, are the network hubs—people like Clendenin at Xerox—whose networks bridge varied cliques and clusters that affect how well you can do your job. These hubs provide and disseminate information, knowledge, and support from different levels and parts of your and other firms that are key to getting the job done. Most of these hubs also provide know-who, that is, knowledge about who to go to in order to obtain the information, knowledge, support, or expertise you need to get the job done. Hubs may even be rich in what I call know-who-knows-who knowledge: They know who are the people to go to in order to find out who is in the know on a particular topic vital to achieving your objectives.

In short, leveraging your personal network means developing a graphical picture of the network, focusing it, and leveraging key contacts to get the job done.

Put Your Organization's Network to Work

IBM used its change management expertise and experts to found its Transformation Unit, which led it to discover that it could use existing social network graphing technology to help bring about change. But the IBM recombination story does not end here. IBM now has taken its expertise with SNA and graphing social networks and turned it into a consulting service that it offers to companies. What is at stake here is not the network that is relevant for a single individual; rather, it is the network of a firm, or one of its constituents, that helps the entire firm get the job done.

Locating and Motivating Employees Leaders and managers who remain sensitive to their firm's or unit's social networks, particularly if they map them graphically, can find many different types of network recombinants. For example, being sensitive to John Clendenin's network made it clear to his superior that Clendenin's network and networking skills could be redeployed and recombined. Mapping organizational networks can reveal many more Clendenins. A sensitivity to networks also helps leaders understand how to help subordinates develop and leverage their networks to become better performers.

The properties of network cliques and clusters can also be leveraged to motivate employees. The army, for instance, knows very well that the cohesion and fighting power of a unit in combat exists in large part at the level of small cliques of soldiers who live together, fight together, and will even die for each other. Smart companies reinforce this naturally emerging esprit de corps in order to empower and motivate their employees. This technique is well known to companies such as Southwest Airlines, which builds cohesive network cliques among its cabin and flight crews that will continue functioning effectively through thick and thin.

Diversity and Trust The properties of network cliques and clusters present a double-edged sword. They can serve as a type of compliance and verification mechanism. Up until a few decades ago, large amounts of money could change hands in the London financial district without formal contracts and guarantees. Yet theft was virtually unheard of. Why? Because the London financial community was a densely networked cluster. It functioned a bit like a small town—everyone knew and could check everybody's business. Indeed, members of tight network cliques and clusters tend to monitor and control each other's behavior and, ultimately, learn to trust each other. In short, clusters like the London financial community leverage social networks as a powerful mechanism to counter employee malfeasance.

The other edge of the sword is the exclusionary and collusive properties of "old boy" networks, of which glass ceilings and race barriers are but some examples. Executives, however, can use network maps to detect both old-boy network boundaries and new types of employees within these boundaries. These employees can be supported and used to further diversity within these networks. For example, one firm I worked for had leveraged the small network of female executives in senior ranks in order to mentor new executives promoted to senior levels. Other companies, such as Xerox and GE, have leveraged informal networks to provide social support for minority employees in their firms.

Forming Teams and Larger Units Leveraging networks can matter most when leaders recombine people to form a team or larger unit. The team in the aggregate must produce the right team-network profile. One executive I worked with graphed employee's networks to create the best cross-functional team—a team of employees whose networks spanned key network hubs in each and every function that had to be integrated. Another executive used this network mapping exercise to form sales teams that contained employees who were already well networked with key decision makers among each of its customers.

Leveraging networks can extend well beyond leveraging the networks of small teams. In many instances, an informal network may provide all the functions of a part of the organizational structure. I will elaborate this point in chapter 7, which looks at structural recombinants, so one example suffices here. Entire industries leverage their employees' networks as sales tools. The examples abound: Tupperware, Creative Memories, Mary Kay, Pampered Chef, Discovery Toys, Home Interiors & Gifts, Southern Living, and Weekenders. Many of these companies, moreover, are busy recombining their direct sales employees with the Web, enabling them to sell through their Web-based social networks as well. Tupperware employees can now host a Tupperware party online, for instance.

Often, the key is simply to let these organizational networks do their job. I have found a tendency in executives to want to meddle with such networks when they realize their existence and their function. Again, less is more here. There are instances, however, when leaders may need to formalize informal networks in order to grow and support them more effectively. I turn to these next.

Hiring Networks and Communities of Practice Chapter 3 examined how hiring often occurs by informal word of mouth, spread through employee networks. Some firms, such as Intel, have formalized these networks so that they provide half of their hires. Paul Hastings, the large California corporate law firm, has taken this logic one step further. It offers attractive bonus compensation to its attorneys who recruit other attorneys in their network. The bonuses are graduated, increasing with how long the recruit stays at the firm. The result is recruiting at a fraction of the cost charged by head hunters.

The role of organizational networks as information-sharing devices is better known. Here too, however, network maps can provide tremendous assistance. The trick is to locate cross-functional clusters and explore whether they are already sharing the desired knowledge. These clusters show up on network maps because they link people with similar jobs spanning different parts of the organization. When these cliques and clusters stand out on a map, they can be (but need not be) formalized and supported with better resources. Even if such a cluster does not appear, it is possible for leaders and managers to divert network piping to transmit a different type of knowledge.

Moreover, knowledge networks do not only span organizations. They extend outside organizational boundaries and have the potential to connect the firm to the press, to government agencies, to customers, and even to competitors. Many companies, for example, encourage their executives and employees to use their networks to lobby government representatives that have a say in issues affecting their firm.

Putting Cross-Organization Networks to Work

Alliances, mergers, and joint ventures create opportunities to recombine networks across two or more organizations. I already mentioned the example of how Corning replicates successful cross-business networks to manage joint ventures. Another example is the use of networks to ease postmerger integration. Indeed, many mergers fail because even though structural mechanisms are created to integrate the businesses, the social networks of the firms are never recombined, and the synergies from merging the firms do not occur. Consider the 1998 acquisition by Rubbermaid of Curver, its European competitor. Ralph Polumbo, vice president of integration for Rubbermaid, decided to map the network of the merged firms in the postintegration period. Doing so made it clear how to detect, leverage, and reinforce the nascent coming together of and the synergies between the networks.

The Sixth Toe

We all know groups of coworkers who eat lunch together every day. Their first lunch meeting may have been accidental—they were thrust together in the same training program and maybe one table was open. Month after month they sit at that same table. As they gossip together, have fun together, and sometimes suffer together, they form cliques that become gradually tighter and tighter. They not only know each other well, but are well on their way to deeply influencing how each other think, what they know, and even what they value and the jokes they know. They also grow to trust each other. They learn to anticipate how the others in the clique behave and to be somewhat surprised when a member of the clique breaks role and behaves unexpectedly.

These lunch groups can be wonderful—the friendship, the trust, the cohesion, the camaraderie. Everybody reads from the same page of the book and fires from the same side of the ship. These cliques and network clusters constitute powerful recombinants that you can reuse, redeploy, and recombine across a firm. Indeed, these cliques and clusters have become more than a network of people: They are networks of people who think and behave alike. They have, in short, formed a culture that guides these individuals even when they are not lunching together. A culture that guides many aspects of how they think about their work and how they carry it out.

The next chapter focuses on understanding, leveraging, and recombining these cultures. Before doing so, a final caveat is in order that applies to both networks and cultures. Though they have many benefits, they also present a threat. Cliques, clusters, and cultures can have a dark side if they are not managed properly. They can become a little bit like those small towns where every one has a sixth toe because everything is a little incestuous.

5 Reviving Values, Not Inventing Them

THE YEAR WAS 1992, *but it might as well have been 1892. The corporate culture of Consolidated Edison of New York, Inc., was a caricature of the culture of firms prevalent during the industrial revolution. Management valued good old command-and-control techniques. It was normal for all decisions to be made centrally. Armies of dark-suited bureaucrats in the firm's sprawling New York headquarters routinely decided everything, from grand strategy to office decoration. For this "HQ brain trust," Con Edison was nothing more than an industrial machine, and employees were mindless cogs who spun out work based on clear directions, the carrot of financial incentives, and the stick of threatened layoffs. Not surprisingly, this culture harbored many informal roles—the employee as agitator, for instance, or the employee as saboteur.*

How did Con Edison become such a living anachronism? We all know the story. Con Edison was a regulated monopoly for decades. Then utilities were deregulated. Con Edison faced a much more complex, dynamic environment full of Enronish creative destruction.

Enter a new CEO hell bent on cultural change. The old culture valued management. The new culture would value a balance of management and leadership: It would be normal, in fact, for employees to empower themselves, to innovate, and to act entrepreneurially to push their innovations up the hierarchy. In the old culture, each unit and subunit maximized its own interest, often at the expense of the entire firm. In the new culture, every subunit would value the firm's collective interests.

To these ends, wide-scale training was implemented at every level of the firm. Recruitment, evaluation, rewards, processes, structures—everything was designed with the goal of destroying the old culture and creating a new one. A few years into this revolution, the results of a survey measuring the cultural shift toward greater speed, innovation, entrepreneurship, empowerment and companywide spirit came in. The survey showed an almost imperceptible change in factors measuring Con Edison's cultural change.

To its credit, Con Edison has persisted on this course of cultural transformation, even through the regimes of several CEOs. Ever so slowly, the new culture has come to life. Today, Con Ed feels, looks, and smells innovative, entrepreneurial, quick to react, and empowered. Yet, the change was extremely slow and cumbersome, and the likelihood is ever present that without sustained effort, the firm will regress to its old topdown culture.

When the cultural change fad arrived on the management scene in the early 1980s, one executive was quoted as saying, "This corporate culture stuff is great. I want a culture by Monday." Research indicates, however, that the experience of Con Edison is much more common: Cultural change by creative destruction is typically very slow—spanning years not weeks, requiring iron-willed persistence by the firm's leadership, and fraught with overt and covert countercultural resistance, often leading to backlashes that drive the firm to return to its old culture.

Why is the creative destruction of a culture so difficult? First, because culture itself is so all-pervasive, taken for granted, and invisible to those bound by it that any attempts at destroying an old culture only end up reinforcing it. At Con Edison, the most ardent advocates of culture change often fell into the trap of using command-and-control techniques in their attempt to destroy the command-and-control culture.

Second, a number of mechanisms work day to day to keep the culture unchanged. What the people in the firm value, their normal ways of behaving, and the informal roles they take on weave together gradually to make up a culture's fabric. This culture often forms, stabilizes, and becomes increasingly tightly woven over decades. Gradually, the culture both shapes and is shaped by other facets of the firm—its processes, structure, people, and networks. As a result, the culture becomes strongly and inflexibly aligned with these other facets.

For example, people who remained at Con Edison did so because they had migrated from compliance, to conformance, to finally conversion to Con Edison values. Those who did not, left. Not surprisingly, the people who stayed resisted attempts at destroying their culture to create a new one. Likewise, Con Edison's incentive systems evolved over decades toward rewarding adherence to its values, norms, and roles. Changing the culture meant changing what employees valued being rewarded for and rewarding them for activities they did not value. Most powerfully, the armies of managers who built Con Edison's culture had to suffer the difficult, time-intensive process of introducing new members to the culture, teaching them the ropes, and converting them. These same managers were often very protective of what they had so painfully created. In general, ripping apart an old culture and trying to build a new culture on the shreds of the past means that the new culture will almost invariably be misaligned with the firm's people, structures, processes, and networks. These misalignments are felt keenly, and both the painful destruction of the old culture and the creation of the new one are resisted forcefully.

Surprisingly, not all changes in culture are as difficult as those that Con Edison endured. Some are remarkable in their swiftness and effectiveness. Almost unfailingly, these changes come about through some form of creative recombination rather than creative destruction. That is, they occur because some astute leader has peered into the corporate basement and found elements of the existing culture that could be reused, redeployed, and recombined to mold something new— painlessly and effectively.

Consider the crisis faced by Mercedes-Benz in the mid-1980s. Its S class of cars were big, bulky, and dowdy and their drivers were affluent, older, and staid—in other words, a rapidly disappearing species of buyers. The strategic goal for Mercedes-Benz was clear as day: It had to make a big stylistic shift in its cars. Even more important, if it was going to appeal to the next generation of wealthy customers, it had to create an even bigger shift in one key recombinant—its culture—both as the Mercedes brand projected that culture to external customers and as it focused the efforts of Mercedes employees. Moreover, the culture shift had to occur quickly, or at least faster than the two to five years most firms take to destroy their old culture and create a new one. And so it did: The company's cultural change was over and done with in a two-month period.

How? To understand what Mercedes-Benz did and how it could be so successful at cultural change, it is necessary to dig into its history. Mercedes-Benz's luxurious, high-quality, flashy, and fast brand and culture came from its glorious auto racing history. Indeed, it dominated Grand Prix racing for fifty years following the company's founding at the beginning of the century until the tragedy of June 11, 1955, at the Le Mans race course outside of Paris. A Mercedes piloted by the Frenchman Pierre Levegh flew off the race course, killing eighty-three spectators and injuring over two hundred. Mercedes withdrew from auto racing for the next twenty years—and its brand and culture drifted slowly from the sporty-flashy to the geriatric-conservative embodied in the S class.

Clearly, the strategic end for Mercedes-Benz in the 1980s was to realign its culture and associated brand image with those of a new, younger, affluent clientele. But rather than undergoing the laborious process of destroying the company's geriatric culture to create a brand-new one, Mercedes-Benz's new chairman at the time, Werner Niefer, opted for reviving, redeploying, and recombining historical values with current strategic ends. During the late 1980s, therefore, Mercedes reentered auto racing, launched the sporty luxury C class, and began challenging BMW's 3 series cars. All this culminated with Mercedes-Benz cars taking the top two places at Le Mans in 1989, thirty-five years after Pierre Levegh's catastrophic accident.

The culture change was smooth. The engineers, designers, and sales force were ecstatic. They were finally going to design and sell cars consonant with Mercedes-Benz's glorious history. In a matter of months, they embraced the firm's return to its deep-seated cultural values, which had never fully died out at Mercedes. These values remained there, waiting for an inspired leader like Niefer who saw that the least painful path to change was to revive these latent values and to recombine them to reach Mercedes-Benz's strategic ends. This cultural élan led to the introduction of the highly acclaimed and successful E class in the mid-1990s that put Mercedes-Benz back into the pantheon of sporty luxury cars.

What did the trick? Simply put, the culture change had a huge impact because it leveraged cultural values that, although they were latent, already existed. Let us now examine what specific elements cultures contain that might be creatively recombined to instill widespread change in organizations, without pain.

What to Recombine

It has become almost axiomatic to believe that companies have a culture. If one listens to the pundits, culture causes most corporate catastrophes, whereas brilliant leadership accounts for successes. For instance, as one senior executive whose firm was found guilty of repeated gross mistakes and improprieties explained to me in all earnestness, unprincipled and unethical executives were not the root cause of his firm's demise—its "culture" was. The culture failed to keep these errant executives on track.

I asked him what he meant by the term *culture,* and what his firm's culture was. The answer was rather vague: Culture was "how we did things around here." In other words, how they did things caused the things they did. The tautology was amusing, but this firm's wide-scale devastation of individuals' investments and public trust was not. Moreover, even though this executive could not define what constituted a culture, what cultures did, and what distinguished his firm's culture from that of other firms, he was certain that the culture had to change.

In my experience, this conceptual fuzziness regarding the meaning of the term *culture* is one of the key obstacles to creatively recombining elements of a firm's culture for positive change. Indeed, how can we recombine something if we do not know clearly what it is? And how can we know we are making progress toward this end, or when we have reached it, for that matter?

There is a Chinese saying that is usually translated as "If you want to know what water is, don't ask the fish" or "The last thing a fish recognizes is the water in which it is swimming." The insight is that we perceive something only when we perceive what it is not. Likewise, corporate cultures become increasingly indiscernible over time to those immersed in them because the culture's ubiquity blinds them to the very existence of a culture in their firm. The only way out of this perceptual trap is either to bring in an outsider who can see a culture for what it is (and is not) or to introduce terms that make it possible to discuss explicitly what is *not* the culture and, by contrast, what it is. Only then do elements of the culture become visible and amenable to recombination.

The Culture Recombinant Framework

Defining terms useful in describing a firm's culture is important, but it cannot become either a navel-gazing exercise or a long, professorial, and soporific diatribe on the subject. The terminology to discuss a firm's culture must be simple, memorable, and, above all else, pragmatically useful. For this reason, figure 5-1 focuses only on three words that denote dimensions of culture that can be changed to enhance a firm's performance: values, norms, and informal roles. These are the recombinants within culture with which the leaders of organizations can work to foster the changes they envision.

Values Values are only rarely the "corporate values" listed in the firm's public relations documentation. Nor are values those heart-warming, inspirational words etched on the little crystal pyramid buried under the papers on your desk. Values do not necessarily help a firm and, in worst-case scenarios, they can destroy it. For example, Salomon Brothers, the legendary Wall Street firm, valued breaking rules—the rules of the market initially, and later, the legal rules of the

FIGURE 5-1

The Culture Map

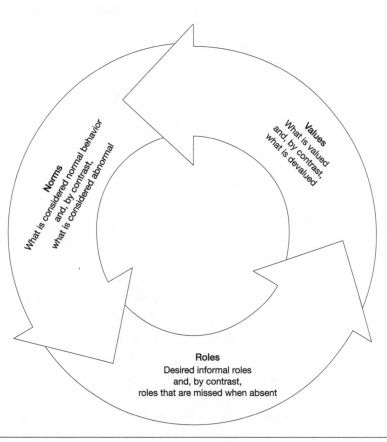

Norms
What is considered normal behavior
and, by contrast,
what is considered abnormal

Values
What is valued
and, by contrast,
what is devalued

Roles
Desired informal roles
and, by contrast,
roles that are missed when absent

game in that market. This led ultimately to the treasury auction bidding scandal that almost brought the firm down.

Values are simply the shared beliefs that people in a firm or part of a firm tend to hold—what they care about, often unthinkingly. We become aware of these all-pervasive values only when we examine their flip side, that is, what these cultural values cause a firm to devalue. When I work with executives to map their company's culture, after discussing the conceptual distinctions between cultural values, norms, and informal roles, I begin by asking them what appears to be an overly simple question: "What values pervade your firm's culture?" Or, if they tell me that their culture is not unified, "What different values pervade your firm's subcultures?"

As an illustration, consider the discussion I had when I asked this question of a group of executives at Sinter Metals, a division of GKN. I knew that this firm had been discussing risk taking, so, to jump-start the discussion, I asked whether risk taking or risk avoidance was one of their values. With little thought, they recognized that their cultural value was "playing it safe."

My next question took more time to answer: "As a result of valuing playing it safe, what does your culture tend to devalue?" The initial answer was more tentative: "We tend to devalue taking risks." At that point, I could make the simple point that we had discovered what I call a *value axis*, which ranged from taking risks to playing it safe (figure 5-2). I explain how to use such a scale later in this chapter. ChangeWithout-Pain.com provides explanations and templates for mapping not only values but also norms and roles.

At one end of the axis are explicit values, and at the other end are *latent values*—those that exist, but are largely de-emphasized. By turning this axis into a scale ranging from 1 to 5, we could locate Sinter Metals' culture somewhere along it. This made it possible to recognize that Sinter Metals was nowhere near a 5 on the playing-it-safe scale— more like a 3.5. On the flip side, the latent value—taking risks—was not so latent. With a little effort, the needle could be moved from a 3.5 to a 2.5. Risk taking would become the more explicit value and playing

FIGURE 5-2

Value Mapping

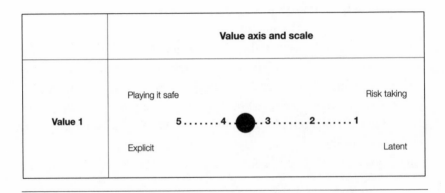

it safe the more latent value. As a result, risk taking would be counter-balanced with a healthy dose of playing it safe.

Norms Whereas cultural values pertain to shared (even if uncon-scious) beliefs about what is valuable, *norms* pertain to shared (even if unconscious) ways of behaving. Cultural norms, in short, are normal, routine, informal, and largely taken for granted ways of behaving within an organization. At one big New York corporate law firm where I once worked, for example, people are largely done with the day's work by 6 P.M., yet many stay at their desks until 9:00 or even 10:00. Employees call it "face time." Face time is the norm that maintains the appearance of conformity to the firm's values of hard work through long hours and its corresponding devaluation of efficient work. Every evening, therefore, it is normal at this firm for thousands of employees to put in thousands of hours of unproductive time.

Cultural norms are invisible in their ubiquity. They become visible only when someone in the culture behaves abnormally. Leaving at 6 P.M., for instance, leads to snide remarks and to charges of slacking off. Of course, what appears normal to most firm members might appear very abnormal to an outsider, such as a new recruit or the employees of a takeover target who are not yet socialized into the culture.

Cognitive values and behavioral norms reinforce each other. Val-ues guide normal behaviors and give them legitimacy. For instance, this law firm values hard work. Behaviors reinforce values—something that is well understood by leaders who lead by example, walk the talk, and more generally use their actions, demeanor, personal space, speeches, and schedules as so many symbols to reinforce certain cultural values and to undermine others.

In the case of the law firm, when the lead partner of the firm decided that the prevailing cultural norm needed changing, he began to leave promptly and very publicly at 6 P.M. every day. In this way, he undermined the old face-time norm and its attendant values of "hard work through long hours" and began to instill instead values of both efficient work and work–family balance.

Informal Roles Informal roles constitute a third facet of culture. Most firms have informal mentors—individuals who will spend untold hours advising and developing a young person with potential, with little

return to themselves other than the feeling of having done a good corporate deed. Other firms are full of informal leaders—people like John
Clendenin at Xerox, whom I cited in the last chapter and whose leadership ability (through his networking skills) greatly exceeds his formal
hierarchical rank. Still other organizations have informal innovators
and product champions.

Not all informal roles help the firm, of course. Certain firms have
informal terrorists who take it upon themselves to sabotage change.
Nonetheless, informal roles and role holders of a culture provide an
often useful recombinant just waiting for a firm to leverage. And that is
precisely my point: Why struggle to create a formal mentoring system,
for instance, when a perfectly functional informal one exists that could
be developed further? (The next section explores in more detail techniques for how to initiate cultural change.)

To recap, then: A strong, homogeneous culture means shared values, norms, and roles that often emerge spontaneously in a firm rather
than being dictated by its leadership to support the organization's
objectives. Values are what is valued in the culture (for example, controlled risk) and, by extension, what is devalued (for example, playing
it safe). Norms are normal ways of behaving, such as either welcoming
or hazing new hires, even though these norms may appear abnormal to
people outside the culture. Informal roles are jobs that employees or
leaders take on that fall completely outside their formal job description.

A homogeneous culture is one in which values, norms, and informal roles are shared widely throughout the firm—an organization, that
is, in which there are few subcultures. A strong culture is one in which
those who share in this culture hold its values deeply, follow its norms
closely, and cast their opprobrium strongly on those who act abnormally—in other words, in a way that violates the culture's norms. The
values of these strong cultures are not just espoused values, found in
PR brochures and unknown to most employees; they are the values
and norms apparent in what people in the firm do, not just what they
say. Therefore, norms and values are more than simply topics for belly-
buttonish fascination, because they influence what the firm does and
how it performs, and constitute a useful lever for both creating change
and for stabilizing its results.

Leaders can accomplish cultural change through either creative
destruction or creative recombination. Whereas the former involves

replacing the old culture with the new—often through a long, arduous, and costly process—the latter means simply surfacing existing latent cultural norms and values and using them to craft needed change with much less pain. Again, it's all about reusing, redeploying, and recombining what you already have sitting on the shelves of your corporate basement.

Finding Cultural Recombinants

In examining cultural problem solving and change, I began first with a means-to-ends instance in which a CEO, Werner Niefer at Mercedes-Benz, detected a cultural problem and then shopped around for latent cultural values that could be revived to solve that problem. Then, in an ends-for-means instance, Peter Browning of Continental White Cap discovered in the course of a turnaround some marvelous cultural values in his firm and asked himself, "What kind of problem could I solve if I leveraged these values rather than destroying them?"

Cultural Means

Before I started thinking about creative recombination, I worked with a prominent New York investment bank that, in reaction to the disclosure of frequent legal improprieties by other firms in its industry, wanted to guarantee that its cultural values and norms would continue to keep it off the front page of the *Wall Street Journal*. Nothing negative had happened yet, but there had been a few symptoms and incidents that were enough to worry the CEO. My solution was to present the CEO with an elaborate plan of cultural change that would destroy old values and build new ones.

His response offered me one of those life-changing moments that helped me begin to rethink the whole creative destruction mode of change. He said simply, "The culture is what it is." How, I asked, did he propose to change his organization's culture if it was what it was? His answer was that many positive values and norms already existed in the firm, and they had kept the organization honest for decades. Building off the existing means in the culture and stressing them, he told me, rather than reinventing the culture, was the surest and fastest way to his desired end of culture change.

We have already seen another example of this technique: the case of swift and effective cultural change brought about at Mercedes-Benz by then-chairman Werner Niefer when he revived the firm's sports car image. Apple Computer offers yet another example of this means-to-ends way of accomplishing painless change in a culture. When, after several years (and four CEOs in succession), Steve Jobs returned to head the company he had founded, he sought to change the prevailing culture, which was sorely lacking in innovation. How did he achieve his ends? By resurrecting an existing means: the company's past culture that incited employees to create something "insanely great." The result was the iMac, an affordable computer with a unique, colorful look that harkened back to the early days of Apple and its innovative Apple II and Macintosh computers.

In all of these instances, the end was clear—change the firm's culture. In all of these cases, the means involved creative recombination rather than creative destruction. All of these cases also rested on finding a strongly held value latent in the firm's culture—an existing means, in other words—and reviving it and recombining it with current circumstances to drive the firm forward toward a new end.

Ends for Culture

Not every instance of cultural change need proceed from means to ends. Another way to find recombinants involves first describing the culture—its values, norms, and roles, both explicit and latent—and then finding all-new ends they can be made to serve.

Return for a moment to the case of Peter Browning at Continental White Cap, which we explored in chapter 3. Browning the master change agent had the good sense to try to understand CWC's culture prior to launching change. What he discovered was a culture that valued resourcefulness, hard work, and loyalty to the firm above all else. He also discovered that these values were more than empty rhetoric—they suffused everything that CWC employees did. In short, he discovered a powerful cultural recombinant.

Rather than destroying those cultural assets and instilling new ones—which would take years for the firm to create from scratch—Browning asked himself what ends this valuable cultural recombinant could serve. When framed in these terms, the answer became obvious. Browning could use CWC's existing corporate values to bring about change quickly, efficiently, and painlessly. Just how that kind of change can ultimately be realized is the subject of the next section, which explores the specific techniques that foster cultural recombination.

How to Recombine

The action techniques for cultural change involve cloning, customizing, or translating to recombine one or more features of a culture.

Cloning Culture

As we saw in the examples of means-to-ends or ends-for-means, crafting change in an organization's culture is often a matter of simply cloning a culture or elements of a culture that existed in the firm's past or that already exist in some other division of the organization.

Such cultural change by creative recombination is a relatively straightforward two-step process. First, recognize the explicit and latent cultural values, norms, and informal roles and map them on value, norm, and role scales and axes. Second, emphasize and reinforce those that could solve problems or create opportunities, and de-emphasize the others. Nothing need be painfully destroyed and recreated.

Take, for example, the value map that I used at Sinter Metals. In that case, creating the desired cultural change meant simply replicating and reinforcing values that were somewhat latent across the firm (moving from a 3.5 to a 2.5 on the value scale). No old culture had to be obliterated. No revolutionary culture had to be invented afresh. It was not even necessary to customize or translate the existing value axes. The trick was simply to emphasize certain values that had been relatively latent in the culture.

It is also possible to clone cultural norms and roles—for example, to stress latent norms of leaving the office when the work is done, or to reinforce roles such as informal mentoring by making them explicit. After discussing customizing and translating cultural values, norms, and roles, this chapter turns to actual examples of how cloning is being used to these ends.

Customizing Culture

Although cloning often works quite well when it comes to creating change without pain in an organization's culture, sometimes existing cultural values, norms, and informal roles may have to be customized to be more easily recombined. An old culture may have to be modified, or it may exist only in one of the firm's subcultures and may need to be disseminated around the firm.

Let's return to Sinter Metals. What I did not mention was that the executives recognized that the playing-it-safe value axis described the culture accurately. Decisions were in fact valued along this risk-taking versus playing-it-safe axis. However, this axis had to be customized to face the new realties the firm was confronting. What was needed was not one but rather two axes, as depicted in figure 5-3. Indeed, what should be valued was not blind risk taking, but rather controlled risk taking—that is, taking risks with knowledge of the degree of riskiness and a contingency plan for controlling their downsides. On the flip side, what should be devalued was uncontrolled risk.

This insight caused Sinter Metals executives to realize that they should not devalue playing it safe. To the contrary, they should value playing it safe when the risks were actually uncontrollable. Similarly, they should devalue playing it safe when taking controlled risks would on average lead to better outcomes.

More generally, customizing cultural recombinants differs from creatively destroying a culture in that old axes are not destroyed and

FIGURE 5-3

Controlled-Risk Scale

Value rank	Value axis and scale		
Value 1	Controlled risk		Uncontrolled risk
	5 . . . . . . 4 . . . . . . 3 . . . . . . 2 1		
	Explicit		Latent
Value 2	Playing it safe when risk is uncontrollable		Playing it safe when risk is controllable
	5 . . . . . . 4 . . . . . . 3 . . . . . . 2 1		
	Explicit		Latent

new ones created. Customizing cultural recombinants also differs from cloning in that customizing involves more than moving the needle along one or more value, norm, or role axes; rather, customizing involves modifying these axes. Customizing norms of face time, for instance, may involve more than making it normal for people to leave the office when the work is done; it may also involve making it normal to come in very early when there is work to be done. Likewise, customizing the role of informal mentor may involve more than making it normal for the many male superiors to mentor male subordinates; it may also require making it normal for male superiors to mentor female subordinates, and vice versa.

Translating Culture

In Japanese, the words for *copying* and *inventing* have the same etymology. Translating this concept of copying from Japanese into English can be tricky. There is no English word for this type of copying that does not produce a facsimile, a duplicate, or an exact copy. Rather, it is a type of copying in which what is copied serves as an inspiration for the copy that results rather than as a carbon copy—something between reproduction and reinvention. The copy achieves the end for which it was designed better than the original, or does so better in the context in which it will be recombined.

This distinction between Japanese and English concepts of copying has two implications. First, it reminds us what we mean by *translating,* that is, creating a new form for something to better retain its significance in a new context. In the case of cultural translation, it denotes reinventing the cultural means to an end so that it can better achieve the same ends in a different culture. The fork, for instance, serves as a means to achieve the same end, eating food, which diners achieve with chopsticks in other cultures. Second, it reminds us that a U.S. firm with cultural values that favor copying over inventing might behave extremely differently from a Japanese firm that has such values. Cloning a "copying" value from a Japanese company to a U.S. subsidiary would require careful translation for the U.S. cultural value to achieve the same end as the original Japanese value.

Consider a real-life example, this one from Deloitte Touche Tohmatsu. This global organization with affiliates in 140 countries faced an interesting challenge: developing a more unified global culture, a common set of values and ways of behaving that could help present a unified image and brand to its global clients and its people around the world. A culture that would homogenize, to the extent possible, the values, norms, and informal roles of practices spanning Europe, the Americas, Africa, and Asia. A culture that would not be valued for its own sake, but rather that would allow DTT to present a common image and brand to its global clients as they interacted with different affiliates around the globe.

The task of such cultural homogenization was Herculean, to say the least. The culture of each practice was already a mixture of the national culture in which the practice resided plus the organizational culture present before it merged into DTT. Furthermore, the images these firms presented to the outside world were quite different from one another.

One solution, of course, would be for the managing partner for global marketing and communications, Adrian Smith, to decree what the corporate values should be, to undermine the hundreds of subcultures in and across the global affiliates, and to enforce cultural homogeneity. Such an approach by creative destruction had, in the words of Smith, a "snowball's chance in hell" of surviving.

Realizing this, Smith wisely decided to follow a simple three-step process of cultural translation and retranslation of the firm's brand image. First, he initiated extensive interviews of close to 10,000 rank-and-file employees and in-depth qualitative interviews, carried out in eight languages, of 200 senior employees in nine key global markets: Australia, Canada, France, Germany, Italy, Japan, the Netherlands, the United Kingdom, and the United States. Second, he defined the results of this research (articulated in English), which revealed several clear-cut facets that the cultures of the vast majority of practices already had in common. For instance, one key common aspect of the culture was the value placed on a "unique work environment," a value described again and again in terms such as *collaborative, flexible, collegial, open, respectful, appreciative of team's unique talents,* and *true partnership.* This was not empty rhetoric; the value was at the base of many cultural norms and informal roles that had caused the firm to win numerous "best firm to work for" awards across the world. A second key aspect was the belief that although DTT is a global organization, it performs better in the local market when it shows, and is proud of, its "local face."

Smith was then in a position to carry out step 3: to translate what DTT's valuing of a "unique work environment" meant in different parts of the world, and what benefits this would bring for DTT's clients and people. This last step was not so simple, however. Even if each of the practices already held this DTT value to a lesser or greater extent, Smith could not simply impose it, or be seen to impose it, on the affiliates. Rather, this value had to be retranslated into a form that would be meaningful to the executives and employees in each of the global practices.

Adrian Smith recounted to me how this was done during a recent trip to Denmark that he made with the Danish partners. The results of the cultural research were communicated to the Danish team. Then Smith asked them to work with him and the European marketing team to translate these cultural values in terms meaningful to the Danish practice, market, and culture. At a subsequent European management meeting in Copenhagen, the Danish team decided to translate and instantiate the "unique internal environment" and the "global organization with a local face" values into a tangible value for their visitors to Denmark. Rather than having a dinner for two hundred people in yet one more nameless corporate center, each Danish partner invited eight of his or her colleagues from around the world to a dinner at his or her house, to meet their families, walk in their gardens, observe their home environment, and then eat a typical Danish meal. This would have been unheard of in certain cultures. In the Danish culture, however, it served as a potent symbol of the value of "unique work environment" that Smith wanted to translate, diffuse, and reinforce on a global basis.

In short, the genius of Smith's approach to a global homogenization of the DTT culture was to begin with corporate values, norms, and roles that were already shared to a lesser or greater extent across DTT practices around the globe. Then, he helped executives in these practices translate these values in ways that made them meaningful and useful in their cultures. Nothing was destroyed and recreated. The culture that existed was leveraged, as were the translating skills of DTT executives.

From Ideas to Practice

Having presented mapping, search, and action tools for culture, it is time to turn to pragmatic questions. First, when should leaders and managers attempt to recombine culture? Second, what tricks and techniques can you leverage to do so? I examine each question in turn.

When Should You Recombine Culture?

A dangerous fallacy exists regarding cultural change. I call it the *mirror fallacy:* the belief that the culture of an organization is a mirror reflection of other features of the organization—its reward system, for instance, or its processes and people. The fallacy is dangerous because it suggests that all that is required to enact cultural change is to alter these organizational features, whether by creative destruction or creative recombination, and presto, the culture will change to reflect the new features. Do you want a culture that values cost cutting, where it is normal to look for ways to cut costs and where the cost-cutter informal role is alive and well? Simple: Just put in place cost-cutting measures and reward the cost cutters. Although this approach sounds simple and has an element of truth, the reality is often much more complex.

Take the example of a senior executive at a well-known pharmaceutical firm I worked for who failed to foster cultural change when he tried to use a similar kind of mirrored cultural change technique. His intent was to take cultural values and norms of sharing knowledge within divisions and to customize them to encourage values of sharing knowledge across divisions. Placing knowledge on an intranet that spanned divisions would mirror itself in values, norms, and informal roles of knowledge sharing across divisions. But as firm after firm has learned all too well in recent years, simply installing an intranet does not automatically mean that knowledge sharing becomes either a value, a norm, or an informal role. To the contrary, if knowledge sharing is not valued and normal before the new IT system's implementation, the expensive system simply goes unused.

In short, mirroring techniques of cultural change often drag on and fail for at least two reasons. First, hoping that noncultural organizational changes will reflect themselves in similar cultural changes can just as easily cause the rejection of the noncultural change and a further reaffirmation of the old culture. Second, as mentioned in the introduction to this chapter, the values, norms, and roles of a culture work day to day not only to constrain and guide employees, but also to keep the culture stable. That's the bad news for cultural change, particularly by creative destruction. The good news is that these very cultural mechanisms can themselves be leveraged and recombined to change the culture without creatively destroying it.

Cultural Recombination in Use

For a culture to persist, two types of mechanisms must exist to counter the ever-present tendency for a culture to become diluted and weakened by external and internal influences. The first is what I call *initiation rites;* the second are cultural forking points in which the organization faces and counters deviations from the culture. The smart cultural change agent knows that these mechanisms will stabilize a culture and make it impervious to change, unless—and here is the trick—these mechanisms themselves are used (recombined) to bring about cultural change. So, for instance, if initiation rites into a culture serve to keep it from becoming diluted by new members, then such rites can be leveraged, customized, and recombined in order to transform it.

Cultural Initiation Rites Every time new people are brought into an organization's culture, they bring with them their own values, their own normal ways of behaving, and their own preferences for playing a particular type of informal role within a firm. Unless these inductees were selected because they have values, norms, and roles that exactly mirror those of the culture (which is very unlikely), they will dilute it. For a culture to remain strong and homogeneous, therefore, there must be certain initiation rites that mold inductees to the culture, rather than molding the culture to these inductees. These mechanisms take them from compliance with a culture they may not understand, to conformity with cultural values, norms, and roles they have learned but not internalized, to commitment to a culture they hold dear and that they have made their own.

People usually think of initiation rites as something that only happens at military boot camps, Moony "weekends," or during a fraternity or sorority hazing. What they forget is that business firms with strong cultures have weaker versions of such rites—usually in the form of an intense induction or training program for inductees to the new culture. All initiation rites have common mechanisms that serve to socialize inductees into their new organization's culture.

First, the inductee into the culture is made to feel that his or her old identity is highly inadequate, in order to weaken it and replace it with a new identity more consonant with the firm's culture. Consider an extreme example to illustrate the point clearly: the initiation rites of

Salomon Brothers, a financial services firm that created a legend in the 1980s and was immortalized in Michael Lewis's classic book *Liar's Poker*. Using Salomonese to describe the process, inductees were treated as "lower than whale shit at the bottom of the ocean." The objective was to turn inductees into a blank slate. This process was as brutal at Salomon as in boot camp. To give the feel, Lewis describes one inductee who was so traumatized by the Salomon training program that he rode the Salomon building elevator up and down for an entire morning, too afraid to get off. The next day, this broken blank slate was gone. Such defections leave those who survive with the feeling that they at least have the right stuff to survive in this firm.

A second mechanism etches the values of the new culture on the inductee's blank slate. During this period, it is essential that nothing intervene to reinforce the inductee's old sense of self. Typically, training programs last from morning until night, involving only inductees and their inductors. The inductee has no time to talk to friends or family who would reinforce his or her old identity. The only influences come from people inside the firm. They bombard the inductee with messages and experiences designed to etch the new cultural values on the inductee's blank slate. At Salomon, this took the form of trips to the trading floor and lectures from one experienced trader after another. These traders had to become the role models transmitting the message of the values, norms, and informal roles unique to Salomon culture. This message also told the trainees that although they were "lower than whale shit at the bottom of the ocean," they were still better than anyone at any other Wall Street firm. Those with the fortitude to get off the elevator and stick it out had the right stuff and could become so-called masters of the universe. The initiation rite was complete: The inductees' identity had been weakened, even destroyed, and then rebuilt into a Salomon identity.

Now consider what happened after the Salomon Brothers' treasury auction scandal that surfaced in 1991. One of the early steps that Warren Buffet took to return Salomon culture to its traditional values and norms of aggressive yet legal behavior was to leverage this training program/initiation rite. That is, he customized it in a way that reinforced values, norms, and informal roles that underlay compliance with all regulatory obligations. The role models who came in to lecture in the program had to symbolize by their words and behavior the very best values of honest business at the root of Salomon culture. Buffet had effectively found a mechanism that stabilized Salomon's old culture, and then he customized, redeployed, and recombined it to bring about cultural change.

Cultural Forking Points The second requirement for a culture to persist is that it must have mechanisms that counter deviations from the culture. Values must be restated when they are violated. Because Salomon violated values of honesty and fair play, these values had to be revived in the culture. Likewise, behaviors must be chastised when they deviate from acceptable cultural norms. At the law firm where I worked, for instance, the day I left the office early, I violated the norm of face time and had to be subtly or not so subtly reprimanded to keep such norms from eroding. Roles must also be recreated when they begin to atrophy or disappear. When one generation of mentors begins to retire, another has to step forward.

For the smart cultural change agent, every deviation from the culture is a ready-made forking point—a timely opportunity that must be leveraged in one of two ways: either to reinforce the existing culture or to change its values, norms, and roles.

Deviating from the culture may mean not only doing less than the culture expects, but also doing more. Consider, for example, the classic story of the FedEx employee who surpassed every FedEx cultural value and norm when, unable to deliver a package to a snowbound customer, the employee took the initiative to deliver this customer's package in a rented helicopter. A smart FedEx manager realized that this event could serve as a turning point in the evolving FedEx culture. It was a golden opportunity to move the FedEx value that packages get there on time no matter what from latent to dominant. It was also a golden opportunity to make it normal to engage in otherwise abnormal behavior to get a package to its recipient on time. In fact, this episode was turned into a FedEx commercial that reinforced this norm and value not only with FedEx employees, but with FedEx customers as well.

Last but not least, I turn to one of the most powerful mechanisms that sustains a culture and that can be recombined to change it—its leadership.

Cultural Leaders and Mentors Almost every book on managing change will tell you that leaders shape and sustain their firms' cultures. Leaders purportedly climb to the top of the mountain, gaze to the horizon, see the future, and come back down and share their vision with the troops who cannot see past the foothills. What leadership and change books rarely tell you, however, is that leaders' work is actually much less grandiose. Most leaders shape culture most potently, and often unconsciously, through their everyday activities.

How does this happen? Let me illustrate. Some years ago, I saw for the first time the then-new president of Columbia University, George Rupp, walking on campus. It was in the fall, his first day on the job, and he wore a raincoat. A small detail caught my attention: a one-inch tear in the coat that had been sewn up. Instantaneously, I formed an impression of this president—he must be a fiscally careful leader. Who else on a university president's salary would wear a patched coat on his first day on the job? As it turned out, I was right. Whereas prior presidents had taken Columbia's endowment from first to almost last in top-ranked schools, George Rupp's leadership was to usher in a period of much greater cost and revenue sensitivity in Columbia University's culture. Between 1994 and 2001 when Rupp left, Columbia's endowment doubled, an increase of $2 billion.

Every action that leaders like Rupp take, every appearance they project, every verbal and nonverbal cue they give off reinforces the culture of the organization they are leading. This phenomenon is not unique to the not-for-profit sector. Sam Walton, the legendary founder of Wal-Mart, drove a battered 1978 Ford pickup truck—whereas the CEO of Enron drove a Porsche. For a person like Walton, who was the wealthiest man in the United States when he died in 1992, such a choice could only communicate to new employees, and reinforce to existing ones, that Wal-Mart was driven (no pun intended) by strong values of cost consciousness.

Moreover, cultural leadership occurs at all levels of a firm, not just at the top. I already mentioned mentoring roles and how they socialize new employees, moving them from compliance, to conformity, and finally to commitment to a culture. By virtue of strong allegiance to a firm, mentors can also be leveraged as powerful initiators of cultural recombination.

In short, day-to-day leadership behaviors not only create and stabilize a culture, but also constitute existing and extremely potent levers to move values, norms, and roles along an axis, to modify other axes, or to translate the meaning of an axis from one culture to the next.

Soft Can Be Hard

The last few chapters have looked at what the soft recombinants of an organization: the people, the networks that interconnect them, and the culture that both constrains and enables what they value and do. The next few chapters examine the hard recombinants: an organization's processes (such as purchasing, production, and distribution) that make a firm run, and its structural mechanisms (such as evaluation and reward systems) that guarantee that these processes recur efficiently and effectively.

In many ways, the work of cloning, customizing, and translating the soft recombinants is more difficult than doing so with hard recombinants, as we will see. The temptation may be to downsize people, to rip apart informal networks, and to obliterate the old culture in order to hire and create new ones. To be sure, creative destruction may seem easier to ram through an organization than creative recombination, in much the same way that it is easier to end a war with an atomic bomb than with negotiations. But creative recombination has the great advantage of leaving survivors. It allows change without fatal pain.

That said, let us now turn in the next two chapters to the somewhat easier task of recombining organizational processes and structures.

6 Salvaging Good Processes Rather Than Reengineering Them

A S EARLY AS *the 1970s, John Reed, the CEO-to-be of Citigroup, experimented with sweeping, rapid changes in business processes. His goal was to destroy an old back-office check-processing operation and create a highly efficient financial services factory. His team used process-mapping tools to design from scratch the optimal check-processing process. Then, one Friday in 1971, they shut down operations. By Saturday, they had completely eliminated existing processes. By Sunday they had replaced them with the new processes. By Monday, they had thrown the switch on the reengineered check-processing system—"the factory," as they called it.*

But by the end of that week, it was apparent that the new check-processing center was self-destructing. The Difference and Fine account reached a colossal (for that time) $1.5 billion on each side of the ledger. Towers of unprocessed documents were accumulating. By the end of the second week, Citibank's money pipeline had burst, and in a case unparalleled in the annals of banking history, the bank failed to meet the other New York banks at the 10 A.M. exchange and to file its federal report.

Citibank's change failed so spectacularly because although existing processes had been destroyed, the new processes had not yet been fully tested and implemented when the switch was thrown. Destroying the existing processes and creating new ones meant that employees had to cope with two time-consuming tasks simultaneously. Removing the old processes meant terminating old employees; destroying existing physical arrangements; and eliminating routines, jobs, reporting relationships, and communication network flows. Implementing the new processes meant integrating new subsystems; writing, checking, and communicating standard operating procedures; training individuals; and starting to shape the new factory culture.

When work started on Monday, they had to add still more tasks, namely, the routine workload of running the system and the additional burden of fighting fires. Indeed, wherever process breakdowns occurred, huge piles of papers and checks accumulated, blocking the check-processing center's operations. All of this amounted to mind-boggling initiative overload and a change process so painful that it was almost destined to fail.

I launched this chapter with a classic example from the 1970s because the bank did almost step-for-step what Michael Hammer advised thousands of firms to do a quarter-century later under the banner of business process reengineering (BPR). The BPR rallying cry was "Don't automate, obliterate." First, executives were told that they could learn nothing from existing processes—which were considered throwbacks to the industrial revolution—and should therefore destroy or obliterate them. Second, they were told that they should invent and implement entirely new processes, without reference to the past. Tragically, just as Citibank's precursor of BPR had failed so spectacularly, so too did BPR in the vast majority of firms that jumped on that bandwagon twenty years later.

Following the publication of Michael Hammer's *Reengineering the Corporation* in 1993, BPR spread to companies large and small like wildfire. A Bain & Company survey of management tools indicates that close to 80 percent of major firms in the United States and abroad had adopted BPR by 1995.[1] By then, however, the management fad had peaked and had started its brutal collapse. The same survey indicates that from 1995 onward, firms abandoned BPR in droves, and the number of articles about this technique dropped from close to 300 a year to below 100 articles, most of which attacked and debunked BPR. Hammer could not stem the tide, even with his 1996 book *Beyond Business Process Reengineering,* and the consulting firm with which he was affiliated, CSC Index, was unable to reengineer itself enough to avoid virtual collapse.

As both Citibank and the BPR fad illustrate, trying to create change by creatively destroying business processes is very destabilizing to firms, very risky, and extremely painful. Even so, in certain instances such big, rapid, destructive changes are inevitable—and not all such changes fail. Indeed, roughly one-quarter of companies that experiment with BPR are satisfied with it, even to this day. A full 75 percent are not, however.[2] Moreover, even where BPR succeeds, empirical research indicates that it tends to create widespread change-related pain.[3] And when it fails, it forces on firms still more destabilizing, painful change to implement replacement processes and get the firm back on course.

Fortunately, there are less disruptive and painful ways to change business processes. Consider the case of a Sony network company I worked with. A little analysis indicated that returned products were greatly inflating inventory costs. Solution: Create a return process and policy. We were hard at work developing the policy until someone pointed out that we were close to redeveloping the same highly effective, tried and tested process and policy used in a sister division.

What followed was a few phone calls and then a few hours of work to customize the existing process and policy. I had come very close to trying to engineer an all-new business process—at considerable expense to the organization, I might add—when a perfectly adequate return policy existed in the company's basement workshop that simply needed to be reused, redeployed, and recombined for this division.

Creating change without pain in business processes can be a simple proposition, as my experience at Sony illustrates. Let us now turn to the kinds of recombinants that business processes contain that can be used in such an endeavor.

What to Recombine

We should begin with a good definition of what I mean when I refer to a *process*. A process is any somewhat standardized and recurrent activity used as a means to attain an end. Processes are often carried out first by people and then recombined to be carried out by machines. Even certain highly complex tasks, such as business education, can now be carried out in part by Web-based applications.

By contrast, business processes are not the same as organizational structure (which is discussed in the next chapter). Structural elements are put in place to guarantee that business processes occur reliably and profitably; they are not the processes themselves. Selling, for instance, is a business process, whereas giving sales bonuses is a structural mechanism to ensure that the selling process occurs recurrently and profitably.

In defining the recombinants for business processes, then, let's return to the same kind of framework or map that we have used in past chapters as a guide for understanding what is available to be recombined. What is needed is a map that can help one detect business process recombinants in a way that clarifies what modalities should be employed to recombine them, what particular challenges can be anticipated, and therefore what tools and techniques might make recombination easier and more successful.

The Business Process Recombinant Framework

Maps that describe a firm's business process recombinants can be as simple or as complex as is necessary. Figure 6-1 depicts a very simple map that distinguishes only three types of processes. ChangeWithoutPain.com provides links to much more complex process-mapping techniques.

FIGURE 6-1

The Business Process Map

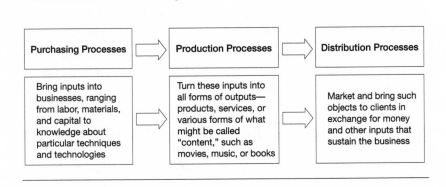

Purchasing processes bring inputs into businesses that fuel their functioning. These inputs range from labor, materials, and capital to knowledge about particular techniques and technologies. *Production processes*—design, manufacturing, and so forth—turn these inputs into all forms of outputs: products, services, or various forms of what might be called *content,* such as movies, music, or books like the one you're reading. Finally, *distribution processes* market and bring such outputs to clients in exchange for money and other inputs that sustain the business.

The key point here is that the three types of processes—purchasing, production, and distribution—can be recombined to create new products, services, or content with often much less pain than if they had to be created from scratch. Let's start with a very well-known example—3M's Post-it Notes. In 1968, Dr. Spence Silver, a 3M research scientist, discovered a process to produce an adhesive made of microscopic spheres that did not stick very strongly when coated onto 3M recording tapes. Silver knew he had found a production process with tremendous recombinant properties.

The 3M employee who delivered on this potential was Art Fry, a new-product development researcher. As a child in a small Iowa town, he had learned how to recombine by turning scrap lumber into custom-designed toboggans. Art Fry saw that he could recombine note paper and the production process for the repositionable adhesive to make Post-it Notes. Since then, other 3M recombiners have recombined Post-its to create products such as the Post-it pop-up note dispenser and Post-it Flags.

In short, 3M recombined three processes to create Post-it Notes, one of the most successful 3M products ever: a purchasing process for garden-variety yellow paper, a production process for a repositionable adhesive, and 3M's standard distribution processes for new products. More generally, many new types of products, services, and content are simple and relatively painless recombinations of existing purchasing, production, and distribution processes.

Finding Business Process Recombinants

As in the case of soft recombinants, two types of search techniques are useful for finding viable business process recombinants: means to ends and ends for means. Means-to-ends techniques involve finding particular process recombinants that could serve the end of solving a business problem. Ends-for-means techniques look at one or more existing processes as recombinable means and decide what end or opportunities they could serve to exploit.

Business Process Means

Start with an end in mind and search for an existing process. The Westland Helicopter case at the beginning of chapter 2 exemplifies how a firm searching for a way to extend its market—by mass producing civilian helicopters—can take an existing process for developing software and recombine it to serve that market-extension end. Likewise, the Sony example at the beginning of this chapter illustrates how a firm can take an existing process—this one belonging to another division—and recombine it to reach a particular end, namely, controlling the number of its products returned by consumers.

Counterexamples of firms reinventing the wheel—that is, inventing processes they already have—are a dime a dozen. As I travel across the divisions, the departments, and even the offices of the firms I work with, I am constantly struck by the amount of laborious, destabilizing, failure-ridden, painful, and wasteful wheel-reinvention of processes that I witness. I also witness brilliant recombinatory feats like those of Sony and Westland Helicopters in which the recombiners go into the corporate basement workshop and leverage processes that already exist. The result in the latter cases is the production of brilliant process recombinations that are twice as effective at solving a given problem and cost one-half as much in terms of both money and pain.

Ends for Business Processes

Post-it Notes provided one example of a firm finding a new end for an existing business process. The pistol-grip drill, which launched Black & Decker, provides another example. It emerged when the two founders discussed drills as a gun lay on the table (don't ask why). In each of these instances, taking a fresh look at existing recombinants suggested a new end that they could serve.

Finding process recombinants often involves carefully scrutinizing processes that already exist and discovering what ends these means could serve—what problem they could solve or what opportunity they could help capitalize on. At other times, the task is even simpler—it only involves discovering process recombinants that already solve particular problems or already help exploit particular opportunities. If you are like me, for instance, you love purchasing new software. These days, almost invariably, the software you need to solve a particular problem comes bundled with all other types of features and software you did not even know existed. This software solves all kind of problems and creates all types of opportunities for you—opportunities that sometimes you never dreamed of and problems you sometimes never even knew you had.

Consider the case of a firm in the off-road vehicle industry that I'll call Sarabar because it wants its name disguised. Sarabar had just laboriously put in place an SAP system. It then discovered that for the system to work, existing structural mechanisms and business processes would have to be customized to fit and exploit the system. What followed was an extensive effort by the firm's executives to develop these structures and processes and begin to align them. The difficult project ended with a startling revelation: The SAP system already contained fully developed business processes and structural support, very much like those that were painfully reinvented. Unlike the reinvented ones, however, the existing SAP structures and processes the firm had paid for were already fully customized to be recombined painlessly with the SAP system.

What's the lesson? Had the firm's purchasers looked at what they bought, they might have discovered the problems it could solve before they materialized. A little more time fiddling, futzing, and messing around with the SAP system and talking with the people who developed it might have allowed these executives to discover some interesting structures and processes bundled with the software. From there, it would not have been a big leap to pose the question: Might these recombinants be of some utility? If the answer did not spring forth at that point, it certainly would have when it became clear that the SAP system had to be aligned with other elements of the firm. Why SAP did not attempt to recombine its IT service offering with some organizational and process consulting services is another story.

The ends-for-means technique of process recombination often can serve to capitalize on mistakes. Consider, for example, the disastrous development process that led to the launch of New Coke—a product that upon its introduction was widely reviled. Because the Coca-Cola Company is a nimble recombiner, however, a few months later it had launched Coke Classic, which is old Coke revived and redeployed to a new end. More generally, firms should ask themselves, Can old production processes be turned to a new end?

We have already seen in previous chapters how soft recombinants can be cloned, customized, and translated to produce change without pain. The following section explores how these three techniques are used on the hard recombinant of business processes.

How to Recombine

As a first step, it is necessary to map out existing purchasing, production, and distribution processes. Interestingly, most of the processes-mapping techniques and software developed by business process reengineers in order to bring about creative destruction can be reused and recombined to bring about creative recombination. (ChangeWithoutPain.com directs the reader to such tools.) You do not use these creative-destruction process-mapping tools to depict the brand-new processes that the change agent will create after the old processes have been obliterated. Rather, the process-mapping tools serve to document existing processes and to find those you can recombine to bring about less destabilizing and painful change.

As a second step, executives and managers have to distinguish processes that can be cloned and recombined from those that have to

TABLE 6-1

Process Recombination Modalities

Recombination Modality	Cloning	Customizing	Translating
Action	Plug and play	Devise and improvise	Juxtapose and jury-rig
Knowledge	Know-what	Know-why and know-when	Know-who and know-who-knows-who

be customized or translated in order to create new products, services, or content. Drawing such a distinction, as in table 6-1, clarifies which types of knowledge and techniques will be necessary to carry out business process recombination.

Cloning Processes

In the Sony example, cloning was the method executives used when they learned of an existing process for handling returned products in another network company that they simply needed to use in their division. Indeed, the network companies were virtually identical in all respects except for their return processes. Therefore, how this return process would interface and recombine with existing processes in the division was extremely clear. It was a straightforward task to clone the process, plug it into the existing process flow, and let it play its role. Virtually no customization was necessary, and none of what I called know-when or know-why in chapter 2 had to be invoked.

The similarity among the Sony companies made it possible to simply clone and recombine a process. Processes built around a common standard present another type of situation that makes straightforward cloning and recombining possible. When common standards exist, it is imperative to leverage them. Let me illustrate this point with another IT example. I was working with a team of senior executives at a large European financial services firm that I will call Marburg Grace because this example is not particularly flattering to the firm. They were befuddled by how difficult it was to recombine the firm's IT assets. With a little analysis, the answer became clear. Their firm's culture valued prompt IT service and therefore devalued reusable IT. More concretely, it was normal for the IT department to be able to procure a piece of unstandardized customer management software in two weeks, rather than taking a third week to give the software a standardized, clear interface that would render it easily recombinable with other software in and around the firm. In short, at least in the case of IT, enforcing and reinforcing standards makes recombination easier, smoother, and more effective.

This type of cloning is not limited to recombining one process. Intel, for example, was dismayed to find wide variations in productivity and quality across its plants throughout the globe. This pushed it to adopt a new production approach it calls Copy Exactly. In 2002, Intel implemented this approach at its Rio Rancho, New Mexico, plant. Such cloning across clear interfaces is easy on the knowledge front. All that is required is knowledge of what has to be cloned, plugged in, and played.

One caveat is in order here, however, particularly when it comes to recombinations that involve many disparate recombinants and therefore many interfaces between these recombinants. Michael Polanyi, the great philosopher of science, gives the example of a high-performing U.S. factory that was replicated process by process, machine by machine, and bolt for bolt to replace one destroyed during World War II.[4] To his great surprise, the cloned factory could not even function. He notes that recombining across many interfaces can require not just know-what but also know-how and know-why (what he called *tacit knowledge*) to get complex recombinations to work.

Customizing Processes

Let's start with an example of customization from show business. Consider the process for generating a James Bond movie script. There must be a twisted megalomaniac hatching an ugly plot to conquer the world and his even uglier deformed bouncer; at least two chases using new types of cool transportation devices; a couple of gadgets from Q for breaking, entering, and killing; hundreds of dead minions and bad puns; a few martinis shaken but not stirred; one evil and one good sexy female object of Bond's special attentions; one Ms. Moneypenny rejection; and one final fiery, explosive moment where both the evildoer and Bond's love interest are consumed and consummated.

The James Bond script-writing process, however, cannot be cloned. The process has to be customized to the current Zeitgeist. It will no longer do, for instance, to cast Bond as a heartless sex addict—in later movies, his character has been customized to make him a painfully romantic sex addict.

Customizing processes occurs not only in show business, but in other types of businesses as well. Dow Chemical Company, for example, did not limit itself to deploying its savvy for recombining and marketing products that were developed for industrial applications (such as Saran Wrap or Styrofoam) to the home products market. It has repeated this market-extension process in markets ranging from skin lotions and shampoos to household cleaning products. Indeed, its subsidiary responsible for such product recombinations, DowBrands, continues to generate successful recombinants such as Spray 'n Wash, Stain Stick, and Freezloc plastic freezer wrap. The process of shifting a production process from one market to another cannot be simply cloned. The marketing process for a general-use product such as Styrofoam is quite different from the process for a special-use product such as sandwich bags. The market-extension process, therefore, had to be customized for each market.

Know-When and Know-Why Recombining by cloning requires limited knowledge, or know-what. Recombining by customizing is less standardized and therefore requires more and varied knowledge—what I have called know-why and know-when.

Consider the example of ATKearny, a firm with strong experience in deploying technical solutions for its clients. Like many consulting firms, ATKearny used to lock up its expertise in what were known as knowledge pyramids, each of which was carefully guarded by a partner at the top and a set of associates below. When a new process was needed to better serve a client, people in the pyramid laboriously reinvented processes that already existed in dozens of other pyramids. However, ATKearny is a very different company today. With great success, it uses sophisticated information-sharing processes to capture, share, imitate, and recombine existing expertise rather than reinvent it. Its culture generously rewards, or should I say mandates, imitation. Key among these structural processes are a bevy of mechanisms that transmit the know-why and know-when necessary to recombine across fuzzy interfaces.

Translating Processes

The transfer and recombination of technologies and technological processes is quite common across firms and industries. Hard evidence indicates, for instance, that 70 percent of technologies developed in one industry are reused in another industry.[5] The process to produce lasers, for example, is recombinable in many business contexts. It has been recombined across sectors such as telecommunications equipment, weapon systems, navigational instruments, textile machinery, and surgical and other precision measurements. Likewise, the laser has been recombined with other products ranging from printers to sound systems and from scanning systems to cash registers.

Recombining production processes often means pulling together completely mismatched parts and making them work together. This often requires more than improvising minor modifications to the processes in order to recombine them. Some processes may have to be virtually reinvented because existing processes simply do not fit smoothly together.

Reinvention is extremely different from invention. Reinvention has the dual meaning of copying and invention that I discussed in chapter 5. Copies are not mere carbon copies—the copy is often better than the original and better suited to its new context. The Walkman, for example, was a vastly superior reinvention of the cassette players that inspired this Sony "copy."

Another example is Northrop, the aerospace manufacturing firm. With the help of a popular maker of pound cake and other food products, it translated a production process used in the sports industry into one useful in the aerospace industry. In making certain fuselages, wings, noses, and tail sections, Northrop had begun replacing production processes that used aluminum as an input with production processes that used much cheaper, lighter, and more durable carbon-composite materials. This meant borrowing and recombining a production process from tennis racket and ski manufacturing industries. However, because carbon materials have to be kept at low temperatures prior to handling, recombining carbon materials with aircraft production techniques required cooling processes that could keep large sections of aircraft at low temperatures. The acquisition process of these materials, therefore, had to be translated for use in the aerospace industry. To reinvent such a cooling process, Northrop engineers turned to engineers at Sara Lee bakery products, who were experts in the process of refrigerating large facilities. What resulted was reinvention that saved the company time, money, and pain.

Know-Who and Translators   A key element in business process translations is *know-who:* Knowledge of who is the person or persons with the expertise to reinvent a recombinant in order to translate its use from one context to another. Who, for instance, could reinvent and translate a cooling process used in carbon-composite tennis rackets to serve as a production process for aircraft fuselages? Such translators, whether they be language translators or Sara Lee engineers, have to understand the properties of recombinants so well that they can reinvent them, translate them, and recombine them.

From Ideas to Practice

Lands' End will help you design custom-fit chinos over the Web. You enter information about your sartorial tastes and body dimensions. The information flows electronically into a computer program that generates your unique design file. High-speed Web connections transmit your design file to a contract manufacturer in Mexico, where numerically controlled cutting equipment and modular sewing setups churn out your very own pair of chinos. Express mail returns your chinos to you two weeks after you pushed the Enter key on your computer. With practice, this two-week cycle time is dropping rapidly at Lands' End.

Job shops used to produce custom products singly or in small batches. Companies such as Lands' End produce customized products on a mass scale through *mass customization processes*. These processes differ radically from mass production processes—those relatively inflexible processes, dating from the industrial revolution, that were designed to produce increasing quantities of the same product or service at a declining marginal cost.

The previous section focused on the simpler case of cloning, customizing, and translating standard mass production processes.

Cloning, customizing, and translating, however, lend themselves particularly well to mass customization and even to what I term *mass improvisation*.

Mass Customization

As customer tastes become more idiosyncratic, varied, and dynamic, acquisition, production, and distribution processes have become more varied and flexible to fulfill this variegated demand. Certain companies have been quick to move to this mass customization frontier, as we saw in the case of Lands' End. Lands' End is not alone, however. Log on to Dell's Web site and you can design your own computer. Log on to a host of other Web sites and you can design your own shoes, watch, toy, vitamin pills, reading packet, car, or motorcycle.

Where does business process recombination come in? Consider the Dell Web site. You order your customized Dell computer, which is a particular configuration of Dell recombinants: a memory module of a particular size, a processor running at a specific speed, a drive with a specific capacity, a display with a specific resolution, and software with particular functionality. The next customer orders a very different configuration of Dell recombinants. Mass customization requires production processes that can clone, customize, and translate varied recombinants and then recombine them rapidly in any number of configurations. Typically, this involves a generic product design—a generic computer, car, or chinos design with which firms can recombine a broad range of add-ons. Rapid prototyping and digital manufacturing then provide the processes necessary to build each custom product.

Mass Improvisation

Consider the high-end retail clothing sector. It changes so rapidly that even mass customization processes cannot keep up. All forms of new- and old-economy competitors flood the market, ranging from every variety of Web shopper and consolidator to foreign entrants. On the customer side, sartorial fashions sweep the industry in ever faster and varied succession, including fashions for dress-down casual attire. Moreover, on the demand side, all forms of electronic gadgets have become fashionable substitutes ready to soak up consumers' discretionary spending.

Industries such as the high-end retail clothing sector that are characterized by complex and rapidly changing demand require the greatest flexibility in cloning, customizing, and translating existing processes in order to meet this demand. These processes must sense and clarify idiosyncratic customer demand and improvise the right acquisition, production, and distribution processes to sell the customer. In these industries, any process standardization can become an obstacle to meeting customer needs, rather than an enabler. Therefore, purchasing, production, and sales processes must have extremely flexible recombinant properties. How do companies do it?

Let's take Nordstrom as an example of a high-end clothing retailer. One Nordstrom store does not have the shirt that Bill really likes and which he "wants immediately, if not sooner"—in his preferred color, style, fabric, and size, of course. "Not to worry," says John, Bill's salesperson. "I drive by another Nordstrom store on my way home. I'll pick up the shirt for you and FedEx it to you tonight—just pay at the counter." To give a feel for the invisible planning that allows for these improvised process recombinations, consider Nordstrom's one-line employee manual: "Rule #1: Use your good judgment in all situations. There will be no additional rules."

At companies like Nordstrom, the key technique that facilitates recombination is what, for lack of a better word, we usually call improvisation. To be clear what an improvisation process is, let's first be clear what it is not. It is not winging it—doing something without any plan. Nor is improvisation extensive planning followed by a long delay, leading up to execution. Improvisation, rather, is planning in the midst of doing. Nordstrom, for example, has a clear plan—do anything, within your own good judgment, to serve the customer. Such planned improvisation is extremely flexible. Initial plans guide subsequent actions, whose immediate results, as well as newly emerging opportunities, serve as a basis for modifying the plans. A cycle of improvised planning and doing gradually brings both into alignment.

What does planned improvisation call on you to find, redeploy, and recombine? First, it means sharing, among employees, improvised processes like the "pick the shirt up on the trip home and FedEx it" process. Second, it requires leaders to revive good old cultural values, like Yankee ingenuity, that make it fair game to reuse, recombine, and redeploy any available trick or technique to get the job done. Third, planned improvisation means relying on employees who can reuse and recombine these tricks *with good judgment*. Finally, it means leaders who do not become trapped by an initial plan and who retain the capacity to switch horses in midstream. Bill Gates of Microsoft, for example, at one point swore off the World Wide Web; a year later he reversed himself. Today every Microsoft product can be recombined with the Web.

Recombining External Processes

Putting ideas about process recombination into practice in mass customization and mass improvisation contexts involves recombining firms' internal processes as well as processes external to the firm. This chapter has already presented a number of examples of the cloning, customizing, and translating of internal processes. I have given less attention to how mass customizers and mass improvisers have begun to discover, leverage, and recombine processes external to their firms. Examples abound, and I can only present a small sample here that pertain to firms that have begun to recombine both their suppliers' and consumers' processes in order to change rapidly, repeatedly, and less painfully.

Put Your Suppliers to Work With respect to purchasing processes, companies can leverage their suppliers' processes as early as the design stage of a new product. Auto companies have gone from using computer-automated design to making the designs and design tools available to suppliers so that they can design auto parts that recombine smoothly with the base design. The general idea involves leveraging and recombining both your own and your suppliers' design processes and capabilities.

When it comes to purchasing, the process starts with a *pull signal*—a computerized order coming in that sets off *lean purchasing processes*. These are processes like those at Wal-Mart, where suppliers carry the inventory and have the responsibility to get items to Wal-Mart when, and not before, it needs them. The basic idea here is to leverage and recombine your supplier's inventory processes rather than your own.

Likewise, companies can rely on Web auctions among their suppliers: They specify the product parameters, and their suppliers bid over the Web for the contract. These companies leverage and recombine their suppliers' bargaining skills rather than using their own.

Put Your Customers to Work   Mass customization and improvisation have also pushed companies to leverage and recombine their customers' processes in order for them to service themselves. The idea is not new. Customers have the process skills to make a salad and to clean up after themselves, so the salad bar can be turned over to them. They can make exactly the salad they want, and access to trays and trash cans can be given so they can clear and clean up after themselves to their own satisfaction. Likewise Ikea, the home furnishing retailer, has customers build their own furniture.

Companies have now translated such "customer-serve-thyself" processes and recombined them in a much broader range of settings. An example is the video gaming industry—an industry whose sales now exceed that of the movie industry. Companies not only sell their users computer games, but also have put their young, computer-savvy customers to work designing the next "expansion pack" additions to the programs.

Take, for example, EA Games, an industry leader with blockbuster titles such as *The Sims Online* and *Medal of Honor*. The latter recombines a World War II story line and gaming technology. In this combat simulation, Allied soldiers fight Axis opponents with all forms of guns and grenades. In the case of *Medal of Honor,* EA Games has recombined single-player games with server-based technology to make it possible for large numbers of Axis and Allied players from around the globe to link up via the Web to fight each other on complex three-dimensional battle grounds—so-called *maps,* in the lingo of gaming.

EA Games does not only sell the game to customers; it also provides free access to software to build the maps and creates competitions for the best maps. The winning maps become part of the next generation of software sold back to customers. In short, not just EA Games, but also companies such as Palm or Microsoft leverage and recombine their and their customers' programming skills and processes to develop their product range.

Companies are also increasingly putting their customers' distribution processes to work. Here too the approach is not new. For example: Put clothing labels on the outside, rather than the inside, of clothing and turn your consumers into walking advertisements for your products. However, e-commerce, sales force automation, and Web sales provide opportunities to translate such "our customers help us distribute our products" processes and to recombine them in other ways.

You work at Oracle Corporation or Columbia University, for instance, and you want to know what books, CDs, and videos are popular in your firm. Easy—log on to Amazon.com and look it up. How does this work? When they purchase a book online, Amazon.com customers provide their zip code and domain name, and Amazon can deduce where the purchaser lives, works, or goes to school. Amazon.com—with careful attention to each customer's privacy—now gives its customers access to specialized best seller lists for geographical regions, corporations, and colleges and universities. Amazon.com calls these "purchase circles." So you look up Oracle's or Columbia's purchase circles and you find out that the top-selling book at both organizations is *Harry Potter and the Goblet of Fire.* Amazon.com is only one of many companies that are finding creative ways to leverage and recombine customer-driven distribution processes to accommodate their customers' varied and changing needs more efficiently.

Structure and Process

As I noted in the introduction to this chapter, structural elements are put in place to guarantee that business processes occur reliably and profitably; they are not the processes themselves. Selling, for instance, is a business process, whereas giving sales bonuses is a structural mechanism to ensure that the selling process occurs recurrently and profitably.

The next chapter examines the recombination of such structural elements. It also examines how structural mechanisms can support the recombination of particular processes. This includes structural mechanisms to find and recombine the right people with the processes; structural mechanisms to reinforce values, norms, and roles in the culture; and structural mechanisms with sufficient flexibility to support mass customization or even mass improvisation processes.

7 Reusing Structures Rather Than Reorganizing

E XIDE CORPORATION, *the largest producer of automotive and industrial batteries in the world, had a presence in 89 countries—that is, after an acquisition binge in the 1990s yielding a $2 billion growth in sales between 1992 and 1996 and a 36 percent share of the global battery business. Nevertheless, this "growth period" yielded a disappointing $20 million in profitability in 1997.*

In December 1998 a new CEO came on the scene: Robert A. Lutz, the former Chrysler president and vice chairman, one of the executives widely credited for saving the auto manufacturer from its brush with bankruptcy in the 1990s. Lutz was an ex–Marine Corps flier with a passion for speed. In fact, his 1998 book, Guts: The Seven Laws of Business That Made Chrysler the World's Hottest Car Company, *extols the virtues of lightning-fast change by creative destruction.*

Lutz began his tenure at Exide by asking around about the company's problems. He learned from competitors and customers that "your country managers are exporting into each other's countries," creating their own price-slashing competition.[1] Individual country managers, on the other hand, blamed falling prices for the company's declining profitability.

Lutz's response to this problem was typically big, bold, and devastating: a major reorganization that would destroy the company's long-standing geographic structure. No longer would business processes serving a particular geography be placed in national businesses with a country manager at the top. Instead, all the business processes related to a product would be placed within broad product divisions, headed up by an executive responsible for that class of products. Lutz's reasoning was that such a product structure would enhance pricing coordination, cut costs by standardizing manufacturing and eliminating redundant plants, and increase the speed of product introduction.

Many of the disenfranchised country managers resigned in protest, but there was no stopping Lutz: In January 2000, the reorganization began. Lutz promoted Dr. Albrecht Leuschner, then head of Exide's six-factory German operation, to take charge of one large product division—the global network-power business unit. Eight million dollars in costs later, five large global product units controlled Exide's various lines of business. As Leuschner recalls, "For six weeks, I was emperor of the world." Why so short a time? Because on the seventh week of creation, Lutz took over GNB Technologies, a large battery maker located in the United States, where Exide was absent. In order to retain Mitchell Bregman, the well-regarded president of GNB's industrial battery division, Lutz decided to make GNB a fifth geographic division. What followed was a turf battle between Leuschner and Bregman over who would run operations in another geographic location, China. Sure enough, Exide had begun the pendulum swing back from the product structure apogee toward the geographic structure apogee—where it began in the first place.

From there, things at Exide continued to deteriorate rapidly. By fiscal 2000, the corporation had a mere $3.2 billion in sales and was posting $136 million in losses, down from the $20 million profit when Lutz first took over. By April 2002, U.S. operations filed for bankruptcy protection. In May, Robert Lutz stepped down.

Whereas chapter 6 examined business processes and their recombination, this chapter looks at the organizational structures that guarantee those processes' recurrent, effective, and efficient execution. Exide provides a good case in point, since organizations often undergo just the kinds of structural pendulum swings that this firm suffered through.

Indeed, we saw another such pendulum dynamic in chapter 1. Joan's unit at Cisco would outsource certain IT functions in order to gain flexibility, then in-source to regain control, and then outsource again to regain flexibility, forgetting the potential for loss of control. Others cut out layers of middle management (delayer), only to then realize their function and to add back layers of middle management, only to delayer again some years later. Other firms decentralize, only to recentralize as a preamble to decentralizing again. Still others divest and use the cash to go on acquisition binges that give way, over time, to across-the-board demergers. Yet others treat their employees like cogs in a big organizational machine who turn out work motivated by the carrot of higher salaries and the stick of threatened firings. Those companies then "empower" their employees, but quickly become afraid of having those they empower actually be in power, so they retreat to the machine-cog model of organizational structure.

Each swing creates a destabilizing, painful gyration that exacerbates every facet of repetitive-change syndrome. Each swing renders employees more cynical. Each swing causes two episodes of change chaos: one when the structures guiding the processes are removed, another when they are recreated and replaced. Finally, each swing compounds the burnout of employees who must continuously run processes while repeatedly destroying and recreating the structures governing them.

Leaders and managers may find some of these pendulum swings hard to avoid. Nonetheless, employees tell me that they find these swings particularly painful when they occur amid a background of already massive change. Exide's geographic/product reorganizational flip flop, for instance, occurred at the tail end of rapid growth by acquisition between 1990 and 1996, a CEO succession in 1998, and during another massive acquisition in 2000. Should it come as a surprise that such firms suffer from repetitive-change syndrome and frequently fail because of an excess, rather than a dearth, of painful changes?

By contrast, consider the example of Microelectronics Product Division (MEPD), a manufacturer of low-power, low-voltage integrated circuits and microprocessors. MEPD, along with seven other divisions, belongs to SMA, a leading producer of microelectronic production systems, precision mechanical components, and watch products.[2]

An increasingly competitive, cyclical, and complex technological and customer market caused MEPD to refocus from telecommunications to the commercial electronic market. The firm's strategy of rapid, market-driven product innovation, focused on low cost and high quality, should have made it a fast winner in this new market. Yet MEPD brought the few innovations in its pipeline to market at the speed of molasses—and when they finally hit the market, these innovations did not fit customer needs. The chief culprit was MEPD's organizational structure—five functional departments, as depicted in figure 7-1.

MEPD's functional structure slowed coordination across interdependent product development processes and rendered it haphazard

FIGURE 7-1

SMA's Organizational Chart

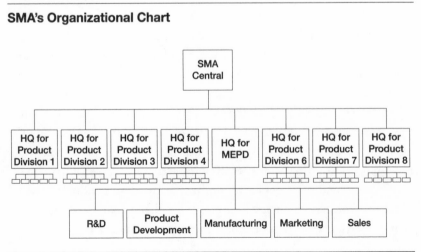

and rife with vicious, cross-functional, internecine political warfare. MEPD cried out for some kind of structural change, creating almost palpable pressure for massive reorganization by creative destruction. That would mean a "reorg" that would swing MEPD from a business divided into functional departments that contained processes with similar functions to one divided up into product divisions that contained all the interdependent processes necessary to create and sell a product. The type of product structure, in other words, that focuses a firm on speedy, market-driven product innovation.

Unlike Exide, however, executives at MEPD resisted the urge to reorganize by creative destruction. They realized that product structures have both benefits (product focus) and costs—two in particular. First, the implementation of product structures mandates a massive, costly reorganization, requiring a protracted period of underperformance before, during, and after reorganization. Underperformance persists until the firm climbs back up the learning curve. Second, as I will explain in greater detail later in this chapter, organizations differentiated into product units tend to be more costly to run than those differentiated into functional units. A product structure shift would undermine MEPD's cost-containment strategy. Higher costs would drive MEPD back, pendulum style, toward a second costly reorganization to recreate its original functional structure.

Realizing all of this, MEPD executives opted to stick with the functional organization. They peered into their corporate basement to find diamonds in the rough—employees who had already begun to act as informal cross-functional product managers. Formalizing those employees' roles, empowering them, and recombining them with the functional structure made it possible to continue reaping the cost savings of that structure while implementing a low-cost, painless, product-focused structural recombination.

How does an organization like MEPD know what kinds of structural recombinants to look for and where to find them? The mapping frameworks in the next section will help answer both of these questions.

What to Recombine

What structural elements can leaders find lying around the corporate basement that they can reuse, redeploy, and recombine to govern processes? To answer that, look again at the SMA organizational chart in figure 7-1. With few exceptions, such box-and-line organizational charts work well to depict organizational structures and to highlight three types of structural recombinants.

The boxes of the organizational chart represent the first type of recombinant: divisions, departments, intradepartmental units, hierarchical levels, and so on. Leaders can reuse, redeploy, and recombine both these boxes and their stacked, pyramidal structure. SMA, for instance, has central and divisional headquarters boxes stacked atop eight divisional boxes. MEPD, one of these divisions, was made up of five functional boxes. SMA retained this hierarchical box structure, and MEPD, rather than creatively destroying its functional box structure, recombined it with cross-functional product managers to render it more customer and product focused.

The second type of structural recombinants can be found in the lines of a box-and-line organizational diagram. Horizontal lines depict lines of communication that leaders can recombine—such as those provided by the MEPD cross-functional product managers. But there are also vertical lines of reporting that leaders can recombine to provide the two-way communication and coordination between superiors in boxes higher up the hierarchy and subordinates in boxes lower down.

Box-and-line recombinants work in conjunction with a third type of recombinant, namely, staffing and control mechanisms. Staffing mechanisms serve to recruit, train, promote, rotate, and lay off people in the firm. Control mechanisms guarantee that planning, measuring, evaluating, and rewarding take place.

The Structural Recombinant Framework

Box, line, and staffing and control recombinants are the materials of structural creative recombination. They are the structural elements that companies like MEPD can redeploy, reuse, and recombine to minimize the pain of structural change and the change roadblocks that pain creates. Let's examine each in greater detail.

Boxes Managers design organizational structures and their parts to guarantee that business processes are carried out recurrently, effectively, and efficiently. Each box represented in figure 7-2 contains

FIGURE 7-2

The Structure Map: Boxes

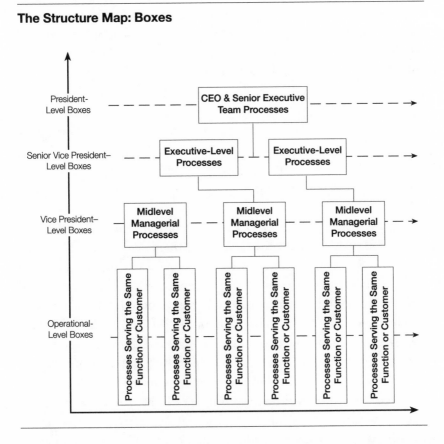

particular processes that are the responsibility of the managers and employees populating that box.

The bottom row of the figure distinguishes two schemes that can be used to organize processes into different types of boxes. One organizing scheme puts processes that serve the same function (e.g., purchasing, production, or sales) in the same box. In the MEPD organizational chart, for instance, all sales processes were placed in the sales department depicted by the sales box. MEPD had what is called a *functional structure*.

A second scheme puts in separate boxes all the different processes that are necessary to serve a particular customer segment—customers who want a particular type of product (*product structure*), for example, or who live in a particular region (*geographic structure*).

Now consider the second and third layer of boxes. Each layer of boxes circumscribes particular managerial processes. The structure in figure 7-2 has three levels of hierarchy (three layers of boxes). A "tall" structure might have five or more layers of boxes; by contrast, this three-layer structure is a flat structure.

The key point here is that each scheme for classifying and boxing up processes—function or customer, product or geography, flat or tall—is a recombinant. It is something that need not be creatively destroyed, Exide style. Rather, it is something that can be recombined, like MEPD did, with other types of recombinants, such as the line recombinants to which I turn next.

Line-of-Communication and Line-of-Reporting Recombinants Firms do not just classify their processes and put them into boxes. They also have lines of communication between people carrying out similar or interdependent processes in different boxes, so that these processes can occur in a coordinated fashion. At one hierarchical level, for instance, the left hand has to find out what the right hand is doing. This is achieved through lateral lines of communication allowing lateral coordination between processes and people in boxes. Across hierarchical levels, the top has to be able to communicate to the lower levels what has to be done, and the lower levels have to be able to communicate to the top what they will do and what they are experiencing as they interact with clients, customers, and the market. This two-way communication and coordination flows through lines of reporting.

As depicted in figure 7-3, there are a number of structural schemes that can open up lines of communication and coordination across people carrying on related processes in different boxes at one level of the hierarchy or across boxes at different levels. All communication can occur at more senior levels—in the senior team, for instance—and be communicated through lines of reporting to boxes at the next level. Another possibility is for one person to be assigned the liaison role of channeling information and coordinating activities across boxes, either laterally or vertically. A third method involves meetings of people in different boxes, such as cross-functional meetings or meetings of superiors and subordinates. Another scheme is the assignment of product, project, or client managers to ensure communication and coordination across multiple boxes. Finally, one can use so-called matrix structures,

FIGURE 7-3

The Structure Map: Lines

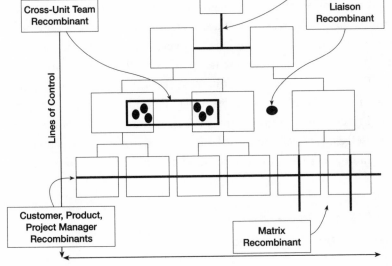

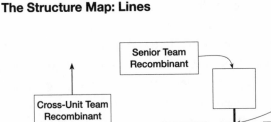

where processes are classified as simultaneously falling into two boxes—a functional and a product box, for instance. Formal lines of communication and coordination are then set up to span these overlapping functional and product boxes.

Each line-of-communication coordination scheme can be thought of as a recombinant, a management-controlled piece of network tubing that can be used to channel different communication content to coordinate different types of interdependent processes. Each scheme can also be thought of as a mechanism that can be copied and reused to ensure coordination across boxes in other parts of the firm.

Staffing and Control Recombinants When people, rather than machines, are used to carry out processes, structural mechanisms ensure that the job is done in a reliable fashion. This requires two classes of mechanisms. The first are structural mechanisms for staffing, which guarantee that processes are staffed with the right people to carry them out. *Right* in this context means people with the right knowledge, skills, demeanor, networks, values, aptitudes, and traits, as I explained in detail in chapter 3. The second are structural mechanisms for control, which ensure that the processes are carried out both efficiently—in a way that maximizes the ratio of inputs into the process and outputs from it— and effectively—in a way that guarantees that the processes generate the right types of outputs. *Right* might mean that the process outputs are of desired quality. Increasingly, it also means that outputs are obtained in a way that is both legal and ethical. Governance and compliance control mechanisms, in particular, are designed with this end in mind.

Figure 7-4 lays out these different recombinants. They include hiring, training, promoting, plateauing, demoting, firing, and rehiring employees. The details of the processes are deserving of a book in themselves. The larger point here is that staffing and controls are recombinants that a firm can reuse, redeploy, and recombine across the

FIGURE 7-4

The Structure Map: Staffing

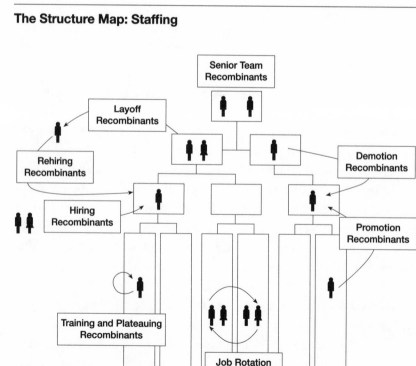

organization during changes. Each variety has its own trade-offs. Thinking of reusing, redeploying, and recombining these mechanisms before creatively destroying them may allow for much less change-related stress and pain.

Structural mechanisms for control, as opposed to the staffing processes just described, guarantee that business processes are planned and carried out according to that plan. As the saying goes, "What gets measured gets done, and what gets rewarded gets done repeatedly." Control processes, then, involve planning, measuring, and verifying process performance.

As laid out in table 7-1, there exist five types of control mechanisms: direct controls, rule controls, output controls, cultural controls, and spatial controls. Direct controls operate when managers plan processes, train or coach workers, and then observe workers as they carry out these processes—correcting their behaviors and rewarding what they consider appropriate process execution. Direct control, for example, is often evidenced by the powerful control that a foreman can exert over assembly line workers, with the resulting loss of employee empowerment.

Rule controls require a set of rules or standard operating procedures governing processes. Managers set the rules and the training to follow the rules and both monitor and reward adherence to these rules. Employees are empowered, but only to decide how to follow the rules.

TABLE 7-1

The Structure Map: Controls

Control Recombinant	Description
Direct control	Managers observe employees, rewarding what they consider appropriate process execution
Rules control	Managers set the rules governing processes, monitoring and rewarding adherence to these rules
Output control	Managers only set targets for process outputs, rewarding employees for reaching targets by whatever means they decide to use, within process limits
Cultural control	Managers shape the culture, and employees are self-controlling and self-rewarding within the framework set by the culture
Architectural control	Managers shape the spatial layout of an office or building, enabling and constraining how employees can behave

Output controls require managers to select or train the right employees and to set only targets and rewards for reaching certain outputs given input constraints. Employees are rewarded for reaching targets. They are empowered to do so by whatever means they decide to employ to reach these targets, including setting their own rules or adhering to none.

Cultural controls operate within the values, norms, and roles of a culture so that they guide employees in making the right plans, executing the right processes, and rewarding themselves often by adhering to the values of a culture they have internalized. Managerial power is exerted only in shaping the culture; in all other arenas employees are self-controlling within the framework set by the culture. Likewise, architectural controls operate when the spatial layout of an office or building both guides and limits how employees can behave. An open-architecture office environment, for instance, empowers employees to interact freely in carrying out interdependent process. To take another example, I walked into a firm recently in which meeting rooms had no chairs. This layout encouraged and forced employees to have short meetings and punished them for long meetings by the leg pain associated with standing up for a long period.

In summary, there exists a rich inventory of structural recombinants that leaders can look for around the corporate basement that they can reuse, redeploy, and recombine to govern processes. The box, line, and staffing and control maps describe what to look for. The next step is to actually find such recombinants.

Finding Structural Recombinants

Let us begin with the ends that MEPD had to reach in its structural reconfiguration, which were very clear: The firm had to place a greater focus on products and customers while controlling costs.

Structural Means

Rather than creatively destroying the existing functional structure to replace it with a product-based structure, MEPD looked around the firm for structural elements that already existed and that could be recombined with the functional structure to make it more product and client focused.

Framing the question in this way brought to light the fact that members of the marketing department had already begun, informally, to coordinate the activities of the other functions in developing products and product extensions. This informal structure could be formalized by taking the informal cross-functional product development coordinators from marketing and, with a little training, recombination, and customization, painlessly turning them into "team-project coordinators" with the formal authority to govern the product development and extension processes. This simple, small, and painless change did the job. By using this method of recombination, MEPD avoided a destabilizing, protracted period of reorganization. Moreover, whereas in the previous five years MEPD had developed no marketable products, in the two years following this episode of creative recombination, MEPD was able to develop no fewer than two new products, ready for market.

Ends for Structures

What unit in a U.S. Army brigade is responsible for defending the commanding officer and his or her command post (CP)? The answer surprises most civilians: the brigade's orchestra. For a soldier, however, it's not hard to imagine some commanding officer asking himself or herself, "What on earth are we going to do with the orchestra when we are in combat?" The orchestra is always close to the CP, its members are trained in both the musical and martial arts, and they form a very cohesive unit that can improvise on a moment's notice, so why don't we have them protect the CP?

This kind of framing of the question (we have this structure; what on earth can we do with it?) is the genesis of all forms of ingenious structural recombinations. Most often, firms recombine in this way because "shift happens"—environmental shifts render some or all the features of a firm's structure obsolete. The resulting structural recombination can range from affecting a factory to affecting a division or a huge organization.

Consider a factory. After the Cold War ended, big military contractors faced declining demand for certain products and excess factory capacity. What could they do with these factories? Raytheon provided one answer: Beat swords into plowshares. Take night-vision goggles developed to help soldiers spot and kill enemies in near-total darkness and turn them into a night-vision system that lets a driver see about

500 yards farther in the dark and avoid killing unsuspecting pedestrians. Raytheon executives estimate that by 2005 the company could sell as many as 300,000 of the systems a year, thereby adding about $500 million to the corporation's $17 billion in annual revenue.

Now consider FedEx, a firm that took its entire organizational structure, designed to serve one purpose, and turned it to a new end. It is easy to forget that FedEx was originally primarily a document-carrying company. Then, "shift happened": In came a series of technologies, ranging from fax to e-mail to the Web, capable of carrying FedEx's customers' documents to their destinations faster and cheaper than FedEx ever could. The company's solution? Don't reorganize—rather, recombine the existing structure to transport not just documents but also all forms of objects, ranging from Grandma's fruitcake to a heart for a patient needing cardiac transplantation.

Now that we've reviewed search techniques for structural recombinants, the next task is to present action techniques to actually reuse, redeploy, and recombine some of these aspects of structure in order to craft much less destabilizing and painful change.

How to Recombine

Structural recombinants, like process recombinants, fall into the category of what I have called hard recombinants—recombinants that are under the control of management. Much of the discussion in chapter 6 about how to use business process recombinants can be applied to structural recombinants. That said, structural recombinations present their own set of particular challenges. Likewise, certain techniques to overcome these structural challenges can be recombined to address process challenges.

Cloning Structures

Structural cloning involves resuscitating, redeploying, and recombining structural elements ranging from boxes to lines to staffing and control mechanisms. This can take many forms. In the simplest of cases— a franchise, for instance—every part of a firm is created from cloned structural elements. Any structural addition to one part of the firm, therefore, can be cloned and plugged into another part of the firm, where it will play its process control role. Spreading such clones to every part further reinforces structural standardization, making future rounds of cloning even easier.

Cloning structural elements, however, is not limited to franchises. A structural recombinant developed in one part of a firm to work with a particular process can be cloned and redeployed in another part of the firm to carry out the same process. In chapter 6, for instance, I described my experience with a division of Sony that was busy inventing a process for handling returned goods only to discover that it was reinventing virtually the same return process operating in a sister division. What I did not mention, however, was that it was possible not only to clone and recombine the return process, but also to clone and recombine the structural mechanisms that made the process run recurrently, efficiently, and effectively—from the measure and reward systems all the way to computerized documents that could be copied and put in use after replacing the name of one division with that of the other. The trick here was to reuse every possible element of the existing return policy in order to reinvent no part of the existing wheel.

Customizing Structures

Most customizing of one structural recombinant in a firm takes place by recombining it with other structural recombinants within the firm. MEPD, for example, recognized that its functional structure focused the firm's attention on how to achieve cost savings in functional processes. This cost focus, however, came at the expense of a focus on product development and customer service. One path would have been to destroy the functional structure (losing cost focus) in order to replace it with a product- and customer-focused structure. MEPD followed a second path, less taken; it retained its functional structure and the cost savings it provided, but customized it by recombining it with a cross-functional line-of-communication scheme that coordinated MEPD's product development and customer service processes.

Leaders do not have to customize box recombinants with line recombinants, as in the case of MEPD. For example, Nokia's CEO, Jorma Ollila, used an existing staffing technique—job rotation—to achieve the same end. When Nokia was at peak performance in 1998, Ollila took the unusual step of moving each executive in his top management team into another executive's job. No jobs were changed, and no one was fired. Rather, each executive was recombined with another executive's job. Asked why he would rotate executives in such a way in a well-performing firm, Ollila answered that such job rotation "helps people learn from one another. Infrastructure can learn from handsets [division] about the speed and product life cycle of consumer electronics. And the phone people can learn customer relations from infrastructure."[3] He had effectively customized the firm's structure by recombining it with senior management job rotation.

Translating Structures

Just because certain structural elements can be cloned or customized does not necessarily indicate that all structural recombinants can. This is particularly the case when a structural recombinant comes from outside a firm's boundaries. It is even more the case when these external recombinants have become fashionable. Moreover, when these fashions cross national barriers, they almost invariably must be translated in order to function effectively.

Take the example of quality circles. This Japanese management technique fashionable in the 1980s consisted of putting employees in unsupervised teams in order to find ways to enhance service or product quality. But a longitudinal study of multiple quality circles in which investigators visited each circle regularly over a period of years came up with one overwhelming conclusion: In every instance in which quality circles were cloned, they failed miserably. But in every instance in which they were reinvented to fit the new context where they were implanted, they both survived and thrived.[4]

Why? Structural recombinants exist to facilitate processes; if the structure-to-process fit is imperfect, then customization is necessary. This is only a partial answer, however. The hard interfaces of structural recombinants must not only fit and attach to the processes that they govern, but must also fit and attach to the soft recombinants with which they are recombined. Otherwise, they irritate the firm's soft immune systems and easily become a victim of organizational tissue rejection. Tissue rejection is less of an issue when a structural recombinant comes from within the firm—chances are it has either soaked up the surrounding culture or already been expelled. People are also more likely to know the recombinant, or to know someone in their network who can attest to its internal origins and utility. Tissue rejection, however, is a big issue in certain changeaholic firms, which have been so overrun with change management consultants that the mere association of their name with a fashionable structural or process recombinant can trigger a violent pain-related allergic organizational reaction.

From Ideas to Practice

Two fundamental approaches to recombining structures exist. One involves recombining one structural mechanism with another to obtain the advantages of both and avoid the disadvantages of each. A second involves accomplishing the same end by recombining a structural mechanism with a people, network, or cultural recombinant instead.

Counterbalancing Structures with Structures

Throughout this chapter, I have been quite critical (maybe overly so) of the tendency exhibited by certain firms to reorganize by reshuffling the boxes—flipping back and forth between a geographic and product structure, for instance, as in the case of Exide. Up until this point, therefore, the chapter has focused on how to keep the box structure unchanged and to recombine with another type of structural mechanism to reap the advantages of that particular box structure and avoid its disadvantages. Nokia, for instance, recombined senior management rotation with its product organization in order to have both product specialization and cross-product synergies across product divisions.

Recombining Lines In the case of lines, as with boxes, the temptation may be to endlessly destroy old lines of communications in order to replace them with new ones. However, just as no one box structure is a panacea, so every new line also presents trade-offs. As firms move from hierarchies, to liaisons, to cross-unit teams, to product managers, and to matrixed lines of communication, they discover that the mechanisms allow for greater communication and coordination, but that these mechanisms are increasingly complex and expensive to run. In the 1990s, for instance, many firms followed the lead of ABB, the large, diversified, Zurich-based company that was then led by its founder, Percy Barnevik. These firms creatively destroyed what were in fact less complex and costly lines of communication to create matrixed organizations and lines of communication that would provide a much greater flow of communication and coordination across these companies. Many of these firms then discovered that the greater communication coordination was not always necessary. Moreover, it came at the cost of much greater complexity in managing these matrixed organizations and at greater expense. Many matrixed organizations have now creatively destroyed their matrix lines of communication to replace them with less complex and cheaper ones.

It might be safer to think of each line of communication or reporting as a firm recombinant. If the line is not wide enough to provide the appropriate flow of communication, then rather than destroying and replacing it, maybe it can be customized using another existing structural recombinant—another line of communication in the hierarchical, liaison, cross-unit, or product manager inventory of line recombinants.

Recombining Staffing and Control Recombinants As with box and line recombinants, each control recombinant presents its own set of trade-offs. Direct controls provide the greatest degree of control but the lowest degree of empowerment. Likewise, as firms move from direct controls to rules, to output, and then to cultural and special controls, they trade off less control with more empowerment. It is not uncommon, therefore, for firms to destroy direct and rules controls in order to put in place output and cultural controls that empower employees. They then experience a loss of control and react by reestablishing direct and rules controls, thereby disempowering employees.

Rather than creatively destroying control mechanisms and replacing them with others, it can be much more useful to customize them by recombining them with other existing control mechanisms to achieve the right balance of control and empowerment. Relaxing supervision and rule enforcement while stressing existing cultural values, for instance, might create a customized control system vastly superior to the alternative—flip flopping between a strict command-and-control style and all-out empowerment. Likewise, customizing staffing mechanisms by recombining them with other structural mechanisms rather than creatively destroying them may allow for much less change-related stress and pain.

TABLE 7-2

Turning Soft Recombinants into Hard Recombinants

Structure	Networks	Culture
Boxes	Clusters of people who discuss a process are cloned into a structural box. *Example:* The Columbia geek clique becomes the Faculty Computing Committee (chapter 4).	Subcultures of people with values and norms governing a process are cloned into a structural box. *Example:* Xerox's African American employees become the Xerox black caucus group (chapter 4).
Lines	Network piping is cloned into lines of communication. *Example:* DTT's network bridges spanning global regions become global structural links (chapter 3).	Informal communicator or coordinator is cloned into liaison role. *Example:* MEPD's informal product manager communication link is cloned into formal link (chapter 7).
Staffing and training	Word-of-mouth recruitment. *Example:* Informal communication network for finding jobs is cloned into a formal staffing mechanism (chapter 3).	Informal cultural socialization. *Example:* Norms of informal mentoring are cloned into a formal mentoring mechanism (chapter 5).
Control mechanisms	Social pressure in cliques becomes a direct control mechanism. *Example:* Southwest Airlines' flight crews (chapter 5).	Informal leader roles are formalized into formal managerial position. *Example:* Clendenin, the informal leader, is redeployed at Xerox (chapter 5).

Turning Soft into Hard Recombinants

The second approach to bringing about structural change by recombination rather than creative destruction involves taking naturally emerging cultural or network recombinants and formalizing them in order to turn them into structural mechanisms. Each of the previous chapters has been replete with examples of turning so-called soft network and cultural recombinants into hard structural recombinants. Table 7-2 lays out some of these techniques and directs the reader to the chapter where illustrative examples can be found.

Pulling the Five Recombinants Together

The technique of turning soft into hard recombinants differs in one fundamental respect from what has come before in this book. Chapters 3 through 7 each focused on recombining only one type of recombinant at a time—people, networks, culture, processes, and finally structure. Turning soft into hard recombinants, on the contrary, involves using more than one type of recombinant at a time. Chapter 8 extends this line of reasoning. It examines not only how companies can draw on the five types of recombinants in their own corporate basement, but also how and when they should venture *outside* company boundaries to find such recombinants in the basements of competitors, suppliers, and even customers.

8 Large-Scale Recombination

SPRUNG LIKE A PHOENIX *from the devastation of World War II, Sony is a company that has recombined itself into a global commercial leviathan, a company that succeeds because it is the quintessential creative recombiner. Why? Because it understands how to make small, incremental changes by "copying" and recombining things that already exist as only the Japanese can—in such a way that the copy ends up being far superior to the original. If you disagree, then compare an original cassette player with the Sony Walkman, one of the most successful electronic products ever.*

Sony's skills at recombination go beyond the art of recombining existing products and technologies to create new products and technologies. It has also mastered the art of recombining parts of its existing organization to bring about change.

Consider Sony's change to a system of networked companies. When Nobuyuki Idei, the dark-horse Sony insider, took over the helm as chairman and CEO in 1994, he kept the existing senior management team largely intact—even the heir-apparent to the top job whom Idei had supplanted. Nor was headquarters completely gutted and recreated, which is often the case during a change in command. Instead, Idei accentuated headquarters' role as the central hub linking what Sony calls its network companies, with responsibility to pick up on recombination opportunities both within and across these companies. Likewise, organizational processes, structures, and informal networks remained largely intact, even after two large structural changes (what changed was not the network companies, but rather the network relations between these companies). Last but not least, Idei leveraged Sony's historical cultural values of reinventive copying, which began after World War II with the Walkman and continued when Sony recombined audio and video to create the Sony Watchman and then recombined audiovisual technology and IT to create VAIO laptops.

Idei's skills at recombination go beyond the art of recombining existing people, networks, culture, processes, and structures within a single company. He is also a master of the art of large-scale recombination—recombining multiple companies with each other. He was the first to both note and capitalize upon the tectonic convergence among what I call the three C's: communications, culture, and consumer electronics, all huge sectors of the global economy. Specifically, he visualized the convergence that could result when communication modalities in the telecom sector became the plumbing through which all cultural content in the entertainment sector could flow into all types of electronic devices in the consumer electronics sector.

Convergence is taking us into a world of computer hookups, through broadband Web connections, to download all forms of films, music, and games from the Internet. Cultural content ranging from film to music, games, art, and e-books flows through communication modalities ranging from phone lines to cables, airwaves, satellites, and broadband. In turn, these communication modalities serve as the tubing to pipe this cultural content to consumer electronics ranging from audio devices to audiovisual ones, IT, and robots.

What companies did Idei have lying around his workshop to creatively recombine in order to leverage 3C convergence? Consider a simplified metaphor for the Sony conglomerate: three legs that Idei could recombine to make a stool atop which Sony strategy would exploit 3C convergence. The cultural content leg is made up of companies like Sony's studios, which produce music and cinema, as well as all forms of film-and-music collages. The consumer electronics leg includes Sony companies with expertise not just in production processes for audiovisual devices, monitors, and laptops, but also in recombining audiovisual devices and IT into products such as the VAIO laptop. It even has recombined audiovisual technology, IT, and robotics into products like AIBO, the Sony robotic pet dog—widely popular in Japan—that can pick out its owner's face in a crowd and answer his or her commands. The communication leg leverages Sony's telecom companies and Sony's skills at partnering with other companies, such as Ericsson in phones, or for controlling by acquisitions the communication tubing that moves Sony content usable on Sony electronics.

The three-legged stool supports a Sony organization producing consumer electronics that users can recombine with Sony content through Sony communication interfaces. Sony communication devices give access to Sony content usable on Sony electronics. And Sony cultural content is available through Sony communication modalities and playable on Sony consumer electronic devices. In some cases, the connection is exclusive: The remote control incorporated in my wife's Sony personal digital assistant works only on Sony TVs, VCRs, DVD players, and game platforms like my son's Sony PS2 game console, which plays only Sony games and can use only a Sony gadget to communicate by broadband only with other Sony PS2 users.

In chapter 1, I used the analogy of my dad's basement workshop to introduce the notion of a corporate basement from which organizational recombinants could be drawn and recombined. In the case of GKN, the company only went to its own corporate basement to find the five recombinants it used to launch Engage. But, extending the analogy, what if an organization were to venture *outside* its own basement and start peeking in the basements of other firms, of its customers and suppliers, even of its competitors? What if it were to use the full breadth of internal and external recombinants simultaneously to bring about large-scale recombination? Sony, for instance, pulled off its large-scale 3C recombination not only by recombining its consumer electronics, cultural content, and communication technology assets but also by venturing outside its boundaries and recombining these assets with those of Ericsson.

This chapter is about the art of just such larger-scale recombinations, which use every possible type of recombinant, both from within and outside the firm, to bring about large-scale changes while minimizing organizational stresses and pains.

Mapping Large-Scale Recombinations

Large-scale recombinations require finding good recombinants both within and without the firm's boundaries—entire organizations that leaders could recombine with their firm, for instance. This is particularly the case with mergers, acquisitions, joint ventures, and outsourcing, as we will see. In these cases, executives can look at a broad range of organizations using maps such as figure 8-1. They are then in a position to decide which of these external recombinants might be recombinable with the firm's internal recombinants. Who would be a good supplier or competitor to acquire, a good outsourcing or in-sourcing target, or a good joint venture partner?

Using a map such as figure 8-1 will invariably reveal many possible combinations of elements that you could recombine. How can you start searching through these many possibilities to detect viable ones? Let's turn to such large-scale search techniques next.

Finding Recombinants for Large-Scale Changes

In 1896, the architect Louis Sullivan coined the dictum "Form follows function." The architectural form of a building should be determined by its function—its utilitarian function, this dictum was taken to mean, not its aesthetic function. There was no need to design

FIGURE 8-1

The External Recombinant Map

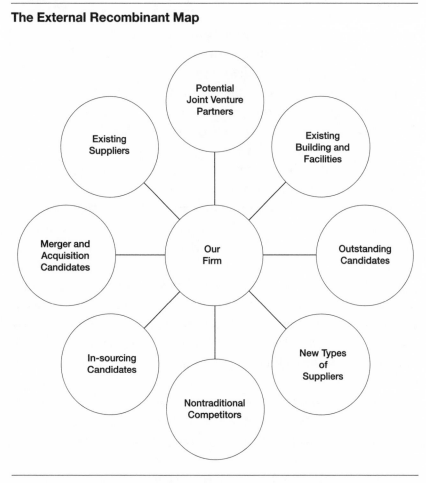

and attach fat little cherubs, or anything else for that matter, to building facades or ceilings if this detailing did not directly serve the building's function. Architects were now free to design business buildings in the form of big boxes pierced by an elevator shaft carrying employees to rows upon rows of cubicles on every floor.

In the context of larger-scale recombinations, "form follows function" provides a better analogue to what I have called in previous chapters "means to ends." Similarly, "ends for means" equates nicely with what I will refer to here as "function follows form." Let us look at each of these in turn and how they can help uncover opportunities for large-scale recombinations.

Finding Forms for Functions

The form-follows-function dictum is often taken to suggest two relationships. First, the form that a firm's strategy takes should follow its function, which is to adapt the firm to its environment. Second, the forms an organization takes—the particular recombination of its people, networks, culture, processes, and structure—should also follow its function, which is to attain strategic goals most efficiently.

What happens if the environment shifts? First, the functionalist dictum tells us that the strategy must take a new form to perform its environmental adaptive function. In Sony's case, when 3C convergence occurred, Sony had to respond strategically and organizationally. Second, the form of the organization must also change to make the strategy a reality. How should this change happen? Sony opted to respond by recombining its consumer electronics, cultural content, and communications assets. Another possibility would have been to take a wrecking ball to the existing Sony organization and to clear the organizational rubble in order to make the space upon which a brand-new organizational combination could take form dictated by a new strategic function. This is the painful, destabilizing approach to which this book presents an alternative.

Only very wealthy nations have the option to wreck a building when it no longer serves a function or when the space on which it stands needs to serve another function. Moreover, even in these nations, architectural conversion is not uncommon. One conversion modality—what might be called an architectural recombination— involves exploiting all the recombinants embedded in the existing architecture for it to serve its new function. In the organizational realm, this would translate into inventorying the full range of people, cultural, network, process, and structural recombinants and seeing how they could be recombined to serve their new function. In chapter 1, for instance, we saw the case of GKN, which needed a new line of business beyond automotive and aerospace. It scoured the firm for any and all organizational recombinants that could be turned to this end. What it found was an informal engineer-renting agency that could form the basis of a new division capable of performing the strategic growth function that GKN executives were looking for.

Finding Functions for Forms

When a building loses its function, the question need not be: How could we use this building in order to serve this particular function? The question can be posed in a different way: What on earth could we do with this building? What possible function could we find for this architectural form?

Consider New York City, which, like many big cities, has seen a dramatic drop in church attendance, leaving many churches vacant. Wrecking them would not only destroy structures of great beauty and profound spiritual significance, but would also violate historical preservation regulations. What function can a church serve, however, other than as a house of worship? Peter Gatien was among one of the first entrepreneurs to find a new function for the church form. After purchasing the Gothic Revival–style Episcopal Church of the Holy Communion at Sixth Avenue and 20th Street for a pittance, he recombined it with a sound system, a bar, and a DJ to make it the Limelight, an extremely successful and controversial nightclub that was popular throughout the 1990s.

Such function-follows-form recombination pertains not only to religious structure architecture, but to religious organizational architecture as well, and to recombining more generally. Indeed, the decline in certain branches of Christianity has presented a major environmental shift for many religious organizations. The Young Men's Christian Association (YMCA), for instance, lost its traditional strategic function when fewer and fewer young Christian men were available to associate for spiritual purposes. Between 1929 and 1933, YMCA Bible class enrollment fell by 60 percent. What strategic function could an organization with this organizational form now serve? The answer: The YMCA recombined itself into an extremely successful nondenominational, not-for-profit community service organization open to men and women. More than 2,000 YMCAs span the globe today.

In short, it is quite possible that an organizational architecture has recombinants that are so valuable that these recombinants, in conjunction with the environment, determine what should be the strategy. Put differently, recombination does not automatically give primacy to either the environment or the organization in dictating strategy. There are many instances in which strategic function may have to follow organizational form. It is quite reasonable to start with organizational form and ask, What strategic function could I perform with this set of people, cultural, network, process, and structural recombinants?

From Ideas to Practice

In previous chapters, I turned to three modalities—cloning, customizing, and translating—that could help organizations actually put recombination into practice. This chapter has to break from that structure. Indeed, multiple recombinants bring together elements of such complexity that they almost always involve a recombination modality that falls somewhere between extensive customization and complete translation. With the possible exception of franchises, mere cloning of an entire organization is infrequent. Discussing the how of multiple recombinants, therefore, is better served by discussing directly how to put ideas about multiple recombinants into practice.

Distinguishing different types of large-scale recombination also involves distinguishing each type of change by creative recombination from its counterpart, that is, the same type of change accomplished using creative destruction—the wholesale strategic destruction of a firm's architecture in order to create a new architecture.

At least five distinct classes of strategic activities at different stages of an industry's life cycle require the kind of change that recombination can foster comparatively painlessly and cost-effectively. The first, entrepreneurial start-up, involves an entrepreneur—functioning outside the boundaries of an existing firm—who recombines existing organizational assets to found a new firm. The second, organic growth, occurs by importing raw resources from outside the firm and using them to grow the business. The third, connecting organizations, is a way to achieve growth through mergers, acquisitions, joint ventures, or outsourcing. The fourth, disconnecting organizations, involves spin-offs, divestitures, or destroying organizations linked to the firm for their assets. The fifth, intrapreneurial start-up, involves an intrapreneur who recombines organizational assets to found a new firm within the boundaries of an existing firm, like Engage.

As in all kinds of change, each of these types of change can be accomplished using either creative destruction (absorbing the pain of

TABLE 8-1

Five Opportunities for Large-Scale Recombination

Type	Large-Scale Creative Recombination	Large-Scale Creative Destruction
Entrepreneurial start-up	*Joining:* Pulling together preexisting environmental elements to form a business (e.g., X-Cardia, chapter 1)	*Creating:* Inventing and creating brand-new elements and combining them in a new way
Organic growth	*Replicating:* Repeatedly copying existing organizational elements and adding them to each other (e.g., Meineke, chapter 4)	*Mutating:* Reorganizing in order to create a new organizational architecture to accommodate growth
Mergers, acquisitions, joint ventures, and outsourcing	*Connecting:* Creating connections with other existing organizations (e.g., GKN, chapter 8)	Absorbing: Dissolving external organizations into the current organization (e.g., J.P. Morgan Chase, chapter 1)
Disconnecting firms, spin-offs, divestitures, and breakups	*Dissevering:* Separating an existing part of the organization and running it as a new business (e.g., Deutsche Bahn, chapter 3)	*Harvesting:* Destroying the existing organization and selling off its assets
Intrapreneurial start-up	*Incubating:* Taking an existing part of the organization and turning it into a new business (e.g., Engage, chapter 8)	*Recreating:* Creating brand-new business in the firm by creating and combining new elements in a new way

destruction in order to create a new organization afresh) or creative recombination (avoiding the pain of destruction by leveraging and recombining existing organizational recombinants). (See table 8-1.)

Joining

Amazon.com and its founder and CEO, Jeff Bezos, offer an excellent example of accomplishing change through joining. To start up Amazon, Bezos simply adapted parts of a familiar bookstore environment to a Web interface. He located Amazon in Seattle, a stone's throw from Roseburg, Oregon, the warehouse location for Ingram, which is the largest retail book distributor in the United States. He drew on the rich concentration of computer technical talent in the Seattle area, attracting only one key player from outside the region, Scott Lipsky, the ex–chief information officer of Barnes & Noble. He then took a run-of-the-mill just-in-time procurement system and recombined the whole lot in the confines of a 400-square-foot garage. Even Bezos's desk was a product of recombination—an unfinished door with four-by-fours for legs. About the only innovation other than this brilliant recombination was Amazon's proprietary computer system, which it developed to interface rapidly with its clients.

Consider a more familiar recombination: Steve Jobs, who partnered with his friend and technical genius, Steve Wozniak, commandeered his parent's garage, hired acquaintances in his network of computer nerds, exploited existing computer technology, and recombined these to form a company—with mom and pop financing the initial bills.

Both examples illustrate how entrepreneurs recombine preexisting environmental elements in order to form a business. The example of X-Cardia, in chapter 4, put particular emphasis on how entrepreneurs like Jerry Sanders leverage their networks as means to such entrepreneurial ends. Contrast these examples with creative destruction, which would involve rejecting everything that has come before in order to create brand-new elements and bring them together in an entirely new way.

Replicating

Creative recombiners operate differently at different stages of an industry's life cycle. At an industry's birth, they operate very much like Jobs or Bezos did. Put another way, at stages of industry formation, recombiners bring together a serendipitous confluence of recombinants such as people, financing, products or services, and customers. In the growth phase of an industry, however, recombiners have to operate very differently. At this stage, the start-ups have already been kludged together or invented from scratch. If the industry is taking off, then there are already a number of entrants in the embryonic industry. The challenge is to grow.

Growth by replicating and recombining does not mean restructuring the firm so that it can grow. It is more like franchising—that is, cloning one successful part of the organization repeatedly and combining each clone with the previous clones.

Recombining by replicating is not limited to franchise-type organizations, however. How, for instance, does Southwest Airlines—a recombination of plastic boarding cards, 737 aircraft, peanut snacks, low-cost strategy, Texas cheerleader–style hostesses, and People Express–type corporate culture—grow from a small outfit with a handful of aircraft and $437 dollars in the bank to the eighth-largest fleet of any airline in the world? How does it do it without an acquisition binge or by mutating into yet another big airline (the creative destruction model)? By cloning the original business model repeatedly and installing it in areas outside the southwest. Once again, nothing is destroyed and created anew. What exists is cloned and then recombined with what already existed, somewhat like a franchise. More recently, U.S. and European mini-airlines have returned the favor and started launching Southwest clones with names like JetBlue, Ryanair, easyJet, and Go.

It should be clear that such strategic kludging by replication differs from its creative destruction counterpart, which I call *mutating*. Mutating constitutes a full-fledged reorganization that destroys the old small-firm organizational architecture in order to create a new big-firm architecture that accommodates growth.

Connecting

Another path to growth during periods of industry expansion involves linking up disparate organizations. This can be done by creative destruction, as in the case of mergers and acquisitions in which the merged or acquired firm is destroyed and its employees absorbed and redistributed throughout existing entities. As was the case in the Chase and J.P. Morgan merger that we considered in chapter 1, the merged firms dissolve almost completely into each other in a creative destruction process that I call *absorption*.

To the contrary, what I call *connecting* is a large-scale recombination that—unlike absorbing—leaves the organizations that are combined largely intact. This takes many forms. Mergers and acquisitions go into a holding company structure in which acquired companies are held under one umbrella corporation. Or they become a multibusiness firm in which the synergies between the businesses are exploited to a greater or lesser extent by recombining people, culture, networks, processes, and structures across the businesses—as in the case of GKN, which we saw in chapter 1.

Alternatively, a merger and acquisition can link firms that have highly similar parts—such as when one company rolls up an industry. Recall the example of Sinter Metals in chapter 5, which presses powdered metals into molds that are then heated, or sintered, to make sintered metal parts. Until recently, small producers made up the sintered metal industry. Sinter Metals used its acquisition expertise to recombine close to one-third of the industry into one of the largest powdered metal suppliers. Existing organizations can also be brought together with much more distant and flexible links, as in the case of joint ventures, outsourcing, and so-called network organizations.

Dissevering

Few industries can grow forever. When the industry reaches a growth plateau, the role of the recombiner changes yet again. Recombining at this stage often involves actually decombining existing parts rather than recombining them. The creative destruction approach involves simply obliterating the discarded parts and selling them for scrap (what I refer to as *harvesting*). The alternative approach—the large-scale recombination—involves dissevering organizational parts from the firm so that they can function as effective recombinations in their own environment or with a weak link to the disseverer. This is often called a spin-off.

We already examined the example of Deutsche Bahn in chapter 3. It faced an environment in which railroads had reached a saturation point; the company thus lost the need for a large planning and project function to build new railroads. Rather than eliminating the planning department, Deutsche Bahn spun it off as an independent company. To add another example, consider the case of RiskMetrics, a recombination hatched by J.P. Morgan, the institutional investment bank.[1] In the wake of a wave of financial scandals in the 1990s that involved Orange County, Barings, Daiwa, Showa Shell, and other financial institutions, Morgan found some of its clients requesting accurate measures of market volatility. In response to one of these clients' request to estimate how much it could lose "with a 95% confidence," an employee recombined basic statistical concepts of variance and probability and developed a simple method of answering this question. This method, as one industry commentator put it, was "so simple that it almost seems ludicrous. The innovation was not the idea or the technology, but in bringing a simple number to the table."[2] In time, this method became the basis of the so-called 4:15 report, due on the chairman's desk by 4:15 P.M. Clients liked the report, so the 4:15 report became the Value at Risk

(VaR) system—a tool used to converse about risk with clients who had little or no financial background. People in the Morgan Risk Management Service group were not blind to VaR's mounting popularity, so they devoted some resources to turning it into a stand-alone financial software product.

Enter Ethan Berman, a Morgan employee who quickly spotted an entrepreneurial opportunity. By recombining twenty-eight ex-Morgan employees dissatisfied with its bureaucratic culture with outside financing, VaR, and new clients interested in VaR beyond Morgan's traditional customer base, Berman created a highly successful stand-alone business. As it turned out, Morgan retained a 22.5 percent stake in the spin-off, which was called RiskMetrics. RiskMetrics—which was free to extend its business to small and medium-size clients and to adopt the small-firm, software company culture fashionable at the time—actually doubled in size within a year, employing more than 400 people by 2001.

Incubating

Recombining at a point of industry saturation involves founding a new business. So the recombiner at market saturation can be very much like the recombiner at industry founding—an intrapreneur, rather than an entrepreneur, functioning within the confines of an existing business and founding a new one. The creative destruction approach here is to invent entirely new parts of the organization and bring them together under a novel architecture. The recombination approach, to the contrary, involves taking existing organizational assets and recombining them to create an all-new business.

An example is Barnesandnoble.com, a highly successful recombination.[3] The leaders of "Dotcom," as it is known internally, believed that with a little borrowing, they could adapt the Barnes & Noble brands as well as its bricks-and-mortar capabilities to e-commerce. Not least of these was Barnes & Nobles' extensive expertise in the speedy procurement of large volumes of books. This capability proved to be invaluable when Dotcom was trying to fill the orders of its e-commerce clients promptly and efficiently. Barnesandnoble.com could also use Barnes & Nobles' extensive back-end expertise in paying publishers, managing inventory, and the like. As Dotcom CEO Stephen Riggio put it, "It's a core competency that we have the infrastructure to know how to do business with all these folks [publishers] and all the back-end apparatus. It's all there. As a result, our online company has been able to hit the ground running."[4]

Adding to these internal capabilities, Barnesandnoble.com has borrowed resources from outside its boundaries: a suite of software applications acquired from Firefly, an extensive list of Internet clients from AOL, and a pricing strategy copied from its new competitor, Amazon.com. What is remarkable about Barnesandnoble.com or Amazon.com is that little is new, other than the original recombination into a highly successful blend of a brand, supplier relations, back-end operations, a client list, and a pricing strategy.

Barnesandnoble.com evolved by opportunistically pulling together a set of people, competences, financing, and clients belonging to Barnes & Noble. Sometimes, however, major recombinations evolve

FIGURE 8-2

Large-Scale Recombination at Different Stages of an Industry Life Cycle

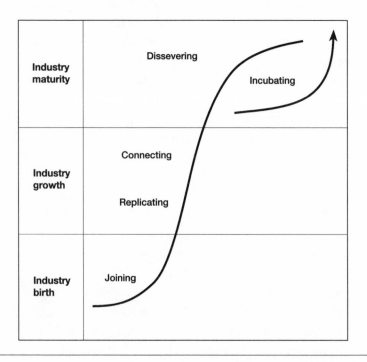

serendipitously with little conscious planning and effort. The trick is not to create these recombinations. It is rather to discover them pre-made, formalize them, and make them profitable.

When to Use Large-Scale Recombinations

As figure 8-2 illustrates, each type of opportunity for strategic change (joining, replicating, connecting, dissevering, and incubating) fits best with a particular stage of an industry's life cycle, and the role of recombiners changes accordingly. However, whether a recombiner joins, replicates, links, dissevers, or incubates, little is created anew. Rather, existing entities from within and outside organizations are combined, decombined, or recombined.

Continuous Change?

Up until this point in the book, I have focused on how creative recombination allows for greater stability in the midst of change, making it easier to approach the change without pain ideal. In the next chapter, I examine another technique to balance change with stability: the general approach of pacing. Rather than achieving change without pain by using recombination to lessen disruption and pain in the midst of change, pacing aims to do so by alternating, over time, periods of greater stability with periods of greater change in order to use the benefits of each to counterbalance the pain brought on by the other.

9 The Fine Art of Pacing

I N THE *1970s and 1980s, after a glorious history that had begun about a century before, Sears faced vicious competition by powerful entrants like Wal-Mart, Circuit City, and The Limited. During those two decades, Sears frittered away its change resources with one failed initiative after another: "store of the future," "everyday low pricing," "brand central," "the store within a store," and so on.*

In the words of one manager: "We got ideas from corporate, but we didn't have what we needed to support them and they were never coordinated with merchandising or distribution. Each idea would come, falter, and go, and in six months there would be another idea. After a while, we stopped believing."[1] Change fatigue and cynicism were thriving. The retailer hit its nadir in 1992, when Wal-Mart and Kmart outstripped Sears in revenues.

Enter a new CEO and turnaround hopeful, Arthur Martinez. Martinez's first years, between 1992 and 1994, were a blisteringly fast whorl of activity, including the announcement of five strategic initiatives, the closing of the famous Sears catalog, the elimination of 113 full-time stores and an accompanying reduction in work force, the hiring of new employees from outside the Sears family, and the decision to spend $5 billion in remodeling to gain additional retail space. By 1994, Martinez declared the turnaround complete. But to the alarm of many employees who had already stretched themselves to the limit during the turnaround phase, Martinez announced that the "real" transformation was only about to begin. There was not even a short period of stability. The next two years saw yet another long list of change initiatives that Sears implemented at breakneck speed.

By 1998, however, the unrelenting, excessively rapid rate of change began revealing its dark side and profits began to tumble. The first clear signs of catastrophe hit Sears in the spring of 1998, when it was sued over the aggressive collection methods it used to persuade bankrupt customers to settle up their balances. This was to be only the first of a series of other problems during Sears's turnaround years. Ultimately the turnaround faltered, and Martinez stepped down in 1999.

As we have seen thus far in this book, change without pain comes from knowing how to creatively recombine existing parts of the firm—elements such as people, networks, culture, processes, and structures that you already have lying around your corporate basement. Clearly, this was a lesson that Sears hadn't learned when corporate was handing down change initiatives from on high without the support or coordination within the company that would be needed to actually carry them out. Nor did the organization learn the lesson later, when Martinez entered the scene with his creative destruction brand of "turnaround."

Yet, based on the sheer relentless pace of Sears's change programs, there was something else that the retail company didn't understand: when to initiate change, and how often. That concept, which I call *pacing*, can mean the difference between failure and success, even for companies that practice the best kind of creative recombination.

Why? Because rather than pelting the organization with one change after another, balancing stability and change allows it to attain superior long- and short-term performance, enabling in the long run more changes, more easily, more cheaply, and with more success. In effect, pacing allows a company to counterbalance periods of organizational change with periods of well-managed organizational stability.

To illustrate the importance of pacing, consider the metaphor of an ocean liner. If the ship is too stable and doesn't roll with the sea, it will be destroyed by the waves' impact. A ship that sways too much and rolls increasingly with every wave, however, capsizes in the first storm, filled with seasick passengers. If a ship is designed to be flexible enough to roll in heavy seas but stable enough to resist being capsized, both the ship and passengers will more likely complete their journey intact.

Similarly, a company that remains overly stable will find it hard to adapt to industry shifts, whereas one that changes with every passing impulse and fad adapts until the constant change rips it apart, hemorrhaging employees who are burned out, change weary, and deeply cynical. A well-paced firm, like a well-designed ocean liner, is able to balance stability and change in order to reap the advantages of both. This does not mean, however, that organizations should remain glued to the midpoint between stability and change—the sweet spot of maximal longer-term performance on the stability/change curve. Over the shorter term, they can drift into the change zone and then back into the stability zone, thereby maintaining, on average, a balance of stability and change within a narrow range.

Why in a narrow range? To illustrate with another metaphor, if you run at full speed on a sunny, windy day, you will get too hot. Stop and the wind will make you too cold. But put on a special fabric used in sports clothing and you will keep your body temperature within a narrow temperature range—neither too hot nor too cold—whether you are running at full speed or standing stationary in the cold wind. Such fabric is sometimes used in fleece jackets, for instance, and is coated with microscopic heat-resistant plastic balls. Run and the heat of your skin will melt the balls, releasing cold that cools your skin. Stop and the cold of wind chill will cause a phase transition that brings the melted plastic back to its original ball-like architecture, releasing heat that warms your skin.

Likewise, truly great change leaders keep their organizations balanced between stability and change within a narrow range around the cusp of the stability/change performance curve. They can therefore respond to environmental acceleration or deceleration with employees who are ready to change because they were spared both excessive change and excessive stability.

Consider, for example, Steinberg, Inc., which in contrast to Sears understood the importance of managing the pace at which change occurred. Steinberg grew from a tiny fruit and vegetable store opened in Montreal, Quebec, in 1917 to a company with sales over $1 billion and such operations as 191 supermarkets, 119 small restaurants, 33 catalog stores, and 32 discount department stores. Rather than the all-out growth of Sears under Martinez, Steinberg grew over a sixty-year period by spurts of rapid change punctuated by periods of rest for the company.

Saul Steinberg, the founder who saw the firm through this extraordinary period of long-term growth, was very well aware of the imperative to balance stability and change. As he put it, "After I expanded . . . I'd always have a period of pause, a year or two to make sure that everything carried and was working out. That we'd be able to cope with the salary changes [and anything else that] we'd taken on. So if you'll study the growth of our company, you'll see that we have periods of expansion and a pause, expansion and a pause." The result of a study completely bore Steinberg out: Periods of rapid store opening and closings were followed by periods of relative stability with few openings or closings, followed in turn by new surges of activity.[2]

Steinberg was able to succeed where Sears's Martinez did not because Steinberg understood the importance of balancing periods of large-scale, rapid change with periods of stability. To substantiate this claim, it is necessary not only to illustrate it with examples and counterexamples but also to clarify why it is true and how leaders exploit the benefits of pacing.

Why Does Pacing Work?

What distinguishes pacing from other techniques to manage change is the emphasis it places on creating periods of stability in order to counterbalance periods of change. The question "Why does pacing work?" is really the question "Why are periods of organizational stability so vital in order to counterbalance periods of unrelenting change?" The answer is not obvious because change theories over the years have given many forms of stability a very bad name ("bunker mentality," for example). Anyone suggesting that change is unnecessary, that sticking with the status quo might be better, or that change would cause regression rather than progress will find himself labeled as deadwood, resistant to change, or a waste of oxygen.

A certain amount of stability, enabled by pacing, works for a number of reasons. First and most important, running stable operations provides ample opportunities for trial-and-error learning—tinkering with existing operational elements, learning the consequences, and doing more of the small changes that improve performance. Such creative recombination through routine, small-scale changes drives performance steadily up S-shaped curves. Extensive research indicates that performance increases slowly at first, then surges at a rapid rate until it bumps up against the operation's performance limits and flattens out.[3] Over this S-shaped cycle, such small changes have been shown to engender massive performance increases in areas such as the aircraft industry, kibbutz farming ships, new surgical procedures, refined petroleum products, power plants, and nuclear operational reliability.

The average decrease in unit costs attributable to learning-by-doing is a whopping 20 percent decrease for every 100 percent increase in cumulative output. Average effects, however, mask tremendous variability across organizations and subunits. One study of Mack Truck manufacturing plants, for instance, revealed a productivity increase of 190 percent over the first year of operation, whereas a study of the production of the Lockheed L-1011 Tri-Star actually showed a decline in productivity. Stability alone, then, does not drive firms up learning curves—well-managed stability does.

Periods of stability to counterbalance change have a second advantage. You cannot reap and exploit what you sow if you migrate every planting season in distant explorations for better pastures. Likewise, companies, divisions, departments, and even small offices face a trade-off. On the one hand, stabilizing operations allows them to exploit the S-shaped returns. On the other hand, changing allows them to explore in order to find a better performance curve. Clearly, exploration is vital for firms. Stability achieved through pacing, however, enables firms to reap the returns from such exploration, as the success of Steinberg illustrates. Constant, unrelenting change does not.

A third advantage of having periods of stability that counterbalance change is that they can become sources of sustainable competitive advantage. Companies that have accumulated long-term S-curve effects enabled by a certain degree of stability are often almost impossible to imitate in their own markets. Consider star performers like Toyota, Southwest Airlines, GE, or Lincoln Electric that have achieved some measure of stability over the longer term. Matching the level of performance they have reached on their learning curves is not simply a matter of imitating their best practices. Rather, a firm hoping to be a star performer would have to live through the same learning process that got these star firms where they are—to relive their history, as it were. Since it would take decades to do so, it is almost impossible to beat these firms—that is, until the environment shifts. IBM, for instance, became virtually unbeatable in mainframe computers until the personal computer (PC) revolution. Personal computers brought all computer firms back to the same starting line in the competition to race up the PC learning curve.

Finally, periods of stability help reduce the pain experienced among a firm's employees and customers. Chapter 1 described the initiative overload, chaos, and cynicism that is symptomatic of firms that practice repetitive-change syndrome, relentlessly imposing one change after another on their long-suffering staffs. What that chapter did not stress is that these firms also become increasingly inwardly focused on change and its disruptions, and decreasingly outwardly focused on customers and their needs. During periods of stability, by contrast, firms like Steinberg spend the time and resources necessary to institutionalize world-class customer service. Customers gain access to a stable supply of resources delivered by the same employees, with whom they can develop trusting and flexible relationships. These periods of stability allow a firm's customers to keep certain aspects of their own operations stable so that they can focus on the changes that they really need to accomplish.

Not every leader has the natural, intuitive feel for pacing organizational change that a Saul Steinberg developed as he progressed in his career. Fortunately, there are tools for counterbalancing change that can help leaders of all kinds foster the brand of change without pain that we've been exploring throughout this book. In other words, *counterbalancing tools* are the action tools of pacing. Let us begin by looking at industries that force rapid change on organizations and considering what tools can help keep damage to a minimum when an organization is going through such a time of rapid change and growth.

Pacing During Turbulent Times in Your Industry

As depicted in figure 9-1, rapidly changing or turbulent industries confront organizations with countervailing pressures. On the one hand, environmental change pressures organizations to make recurrent high-speed changes. On the other hand, recurrent high-speed organizational change erodes the capacity of organizations to change at this

FIGURE 9-1

Counterbalancing Rapid Industry Change

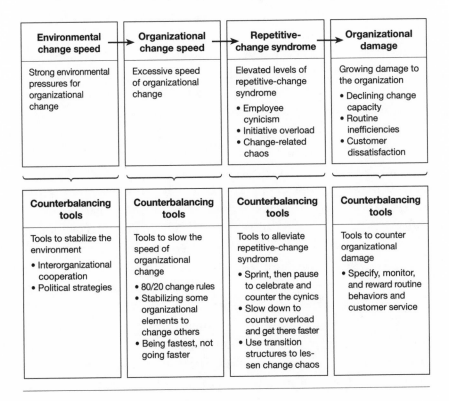

speed. For example, Cisco (see chapter 1) had to provide the infra-structure of the growing World Wide Web. But it had to do so without getting hurt by the unrelenting pace of organizational change—something it was slow to master.

These kinds of countervailing pressures make protracted periods of rapid industry growth and change the hardest to manage when it comes to counterbalancing change with stability. Skilled change leaders take advantage of every one of the counterbalancing tools listed in figure 9-1, which the following sections explore in detail.

Tools for Stabilizing Environments

There is an argument that goes something like this: Executives are not interested in maximizing shareholder wealth, but rather in maintaining a stable environment and minimizing the pain, risk of failure, and personal job loss that frequently accompany change. The oldest approach to achieving environmental stability, the argument continues, is to dominate one's industry so as not to have to change in order to adapt to it. This quest for stability explains why the railroads formed trusts and cartels in the early twentieth century—to reduce the level of change forced on them by interrailroad rivalry. It also explains why Microsoft is struggling with antitrust litigation today, because by controlling competitors it could face a more stable software industry, requiring less adaptive change from Microsoft. In short, no environmental change, no organizational pain.

Why is a stable corporate environment more important than profitability? Because the former guarantees the latter. Not only does stability eliminate the risk of change failure, but it also makes it possible to design the business to maximize profitability rather than flexibility. Organizations that follow this approach are built to accommodate invariant inputs from a stable environment and to return the same products, services, or outputs to the same customers at a declining marginal cost. These companies can be built in the form of organizational machines by engineerlike leaders.

What does this type of environmental stabilization strategy involve? First, keeping industry competition and change at a minimum, rather than changing the organization to adapt continuously to competitive threats in its external environment. Examples include a variety of anticompetitive strategies, such as price fixing. Clearly, these forms of environmental stabilization are illegal and unacceptable. However, many stabilization strategies are not, because they do not harm competition. These include strategies such as joint ventures and alliances, as well as all forms of cooperation with competitors. In chapter 3, for instance, we saw how over thirty firms pooled their job boards to form DirectEmployers.com in order to stabilize their recruiting environment. Nor is it true that such environmental stabilization strategies are only open to large organizations with the power to control their environments. Smaller, weaker firms can often effectively band together in order to stabilize their environments collectively, as in the case of the challenge mounted by Airbus against Boeing over the last decade.

A second type of stabilization strategy is for a firm to move to a stable niche in its industry. Lincoln Electric, for example, is a company that has remained stable and successful for close to a century. It has found a persistent niche in commodity arc-welding products and adopted a hard-to-imitate combination of incentives and employee security, bound tightly together by values of fairness in the distribution of wealth and decision-making authority. Not every firm can remain as stable as Lincoln Electric, and the company's continual placidness actually became a drawback when it decided to experiment with information technology and to go fully global. The period of organizational stability during Lincoln's long-term placid regime was not well managed, making it difficult to implement these changes when Lincoln's environment forced them onto the firm.

Nonetheless, Lincoln demonstrates how a buffering stabilization strategy involves finding more stable niches in otherwise highly turbulent markets. It includes developing hard-to-imitate core competencies in order to engender sustainable competitive advantages. Finally, the strategy protects the organization not only from market shifts but also from shifts in management fashion and the pressure to try each passing fad.

Tools to Slow the Speed of Organizational Change

Three techniques can help leaders to slow down organizational change while keeping up with environmental pressures to make such changes. Let us examine each in turn.

Treating Change as a Precious Commodity Pacing treats organizational change as an extremely precious commodity. It is precious not only because it is essential that firms undergo organizational change to adapt to environmental changes, but also because change can be painful, easily wasted, and in short supply in turbulent environments.

In firms changing at high rates of speed, often well above those mandated by their environments, the acid test needs to be, Does the pain of making this change exceed its benefits? When I walk into firms suffering from excessive change, my strong impression is that only 20 percent of the change initiatives in progress deliver 80 percent of the changes necessary to adapt firms to their environments. The other 80 percent make up 100 percent of the initiative overload.

One common cause of change waste comes from improper planning tools. These tools make it possible to forget that, particularly in turbulent environments, deciding what change initiatives to implement is, at most, only half of strategizing, planning, or goal setting. The other half has nothing to do with what will be done, and everything to do with what will *not* be done. This means at minimum clearly specifying what mistakenly might be thought helpful to reach the objectives. Much more important, it involves clearly specifying what change initiatives will help achieve objectives that are not worth carrying out. That is, what are the initiatives that belong to the 80 percent of change initiatives that will deliver only 20 percent of the useful change results? Finally, it involves clearly specifying what will not change. Too often companies throw out the baby with the bath water. To return to the Continental White Cap example that we first examined in chapter 3, when Peter Browning launched change at CWC, it was very clear what would not change—the strong values of company loyalty, the non-unionized work force, and CWC's reputation among its customers.

Changing Different Organizational Parts at Different Speeds It is a paradox of organizational change that certain parts of a company have to remain unchanged, or at least change at a slow pace, so that others can change effectively at a rapid pace. At a very minimum, the people who carry out a change have to remain the same from day to day.

Organizations that have to change a lot are therefore a bit like mountain climbers. They would fall to their death if they tried to change the position of all their limbs simultaneously. Instead, they must keep a stable base with two legs and one hand so that they can safely change the position of the other hand. Likewise, organizations that excel at change know that they have to hold down the rate of change in certain areas of the organization so that they can change swiftly in another. If a company wants to stay on top of the mountain, not everything can change rapidly and simultaneously.

Take, for example, Nintendo, which holds 99 percent of the market in handheld video games, an extremely dynamic industry in which there has been no shortage of challengers. Its star product, the Game Boy, is one of the most profitable consumer electronic devices ever produced, with sales of $1.2 billion in 1999 alone. Now consider that the only notable change made to the Game Boy's hardware in its ten-year history is that it was shrunk by a few inches to make it more portable, and colors were added to replace the old drab gray casing. This in the toy industry, which is notable for its extremely rapid rate of change. Does this mean that Nintendo is resistant to change? Absolutely not. Keeping change at a slow pace in its product's hardware has enabled it to deploy all its resources to change software at a rate sufficient to outrun the competition. It has changed swiftly to come up with games that could attract thousands of players to its hardware, the most recent example being its best-selling Pokemon games introduced in 1999.

Some firms go so far as to outsource stable aspects of their operations so that they can focus all their energy on those that need to change. Nike, for example, in-sources the highly dynamic design and marketing aspects of its organization, while outsourcing more stable aspects, such as production. Other successful change masters keep the human aspects of their organizations' change at a slower rate so that they can change other aspects more rapidly. Strategy will change frequently, for instance, but the organization, which was set up for flexibility in the first place, alters at quite a slow pace.

Being Fastest, Not Going Faster Companies in rapidly changing environments can easily forget the importance of slowing down and of making fewer changes. Remember the old story of the two unfortunate campers in Africa who noticed a jaguar stalking them in the jungle: One camper sat down and put on his running shoes. The other looked at him incredulously. "You're crazy," he said. "You're never going to outrun that jaguar." "I don't need to," the first replied. "I only need to outrun you."

There is an argument that firms, not knowing how fast their competitors are changing, should maintain the highest speed of change possible. The question is, What is "possible" in a turbulent environment in which it will not be possible to continue running at full speed? A more cautious approach might be to go faster than the competition, even if the speed of change is less than what the firm could achieve at that moment.

Continuous high-speed change, then, is not necessarily the best way to win the race. Consider the example of Nestlé. Listen to its CEO, Peter Brabeck: "Big, dramatic change is fine for a crisis. If you come in as a CEO and a turnaround is necessary, then fine, have a revolution. . . . But not every company in the world is in a crisis all the time. . . . You cannot underestimate the traumatic impact of abrupt change, the fear it provokes in people, the demands it makes on management's time."[4] For Brabeck, all-out, large-scale creative destruction is not only something to be avoided, it is a clear indication that change is being mismanaged. As he puts it, "Frankly, you could make the case that any kind of onetime change program is actually a very worrisome warning. It's a bad sign that a company's leaders have to make such an intervention. Think of medicine again. If you take preventive care of your health, and you've taken the time for check-ups, you won't wake up one day to find out that you have to cut off your leg."[5]

Tools for Countering Repetitive-Change Syndrome

Firms may be unable to control either the speed of environmental change or the speed of organizational change. In such instances, the goal has to be to minimize the extent to which recurrent change engenders the three facets of repetitive-change syndrome: change-related chaos, employee cynicism, and initiative overload.

Fighting Cynicism and Initiative Overload Should you work at a slow, steady pace all seven days of the week, week after week, or should you work harder during the week so that you can relax during the weekend and occasionally take a vacation? Clearly, the answer is the latter. Even the creator paused on the seventh day. For our own mental and physical health, we all need to take at least one day off during weekends, and we have to take vacations once in a while.

Likewise, organizations must learn to speed up change so that they have an opportunity to then slow down, or even pause, as opposed to changing continuously. This is the "work hard, play hard" mentality that I see repeatedly in organizations that are adept at maintaining high average rates of change over the longer run.

Moreover, periods of organizational rest have to be carefully managed—scheduled and adhered to. As the example of Steinberg demonstrates, this kind of organizational "interval training" can be particularly well suited to turbulent regimes and is an important mechanism used in pacing.

Slowing Down to Get There Quicker A Korean proverb, loosely translated, says, "It is when you are in a rush that you have to slow down." This does not only mean that rushing change, under pressure, leads to mistakes. It also means that the same change, implemented more slowly, might actually be completed more quickly—with less disruption and with a greater capacity to launch the next change. Indeed, a slower pace makes it possible to preserve and even enhance the capacity to change if another sprint becomes necessary.

To some this may seem like heresy. Should not changes be implemented as quickly as possible in order to stay ahead of the competition that, undoubtedly, is also trying to change as quickly as possible? Yes, of course, but there are two caveats.

A firm's change capacity is equivalent to the red line on a car's tachometer. It is the maximal rate at which the firm's change engine can operate without causing the type of repetitive-change syndrome that damages this engine of change. So, first, a company has to have the change capacity to pull off the next sprint. Even the athlete who first broke the four-minute mile did not run two four-minute miles in a row. Doing so could have caused muscle damage that would have permanently harmed his capacity to run again.

Second, making this change must not deplete human change resources to the point where the next, more important change cannot be implemented. Olympic runners, remember, do not run one race to get the gold—they run a series of elimination races that they have to dominate if they are to be runners in the gold medal round. They have to run fast enough to win each elimination race, but not so fast as to have nothing left for the final gold, silver, or bronze prize.

Tools for Countering Organizational Damage

Some firms cannot slow the speed of either environmental or organizational change. Nor can they minimize the extent to which recurrent change engenders the three facets of repetitive-change syndrome. However, they can mitigate the harm this syndrome causes to the organization, that is, declining change capacity, routine inefficiencies, and customer dissatisfaction.

The key here is to specify acceptable levels of the three facets of repetitive-change syndrome (change-related chaos, initiative overload, and cynicism or burnout) below which the firm cannot decline. It is then critical to monitor these metrics during periods of environmental turbulence and to take action well before these minimum thresholds have been crossed. ChangeWithoutPain.com directs the reader to such metrics.

For example, I worked with a large European financial services firm, Marburg Grace, which had merged three times in as many years. An employee survey of one of the firm's major businesses carried out during the third merger indicated that after the unrelenting pain caused by the previous two mergers, only 18 percent of employees were satisfied with their work, and in excess of half of the employees expected to move voluntarily to another firm within the next two years. Customers were also up in arms, not only because of the rude service they were beginning to receive from tired, frustrated, and cynical employees, but also because the firm's internal needs to manage relentless change clearly had gained priority over customer needs. With twenty-twenty hindsight, it is very clear that such employee and customer surveys should not have waited until the third merger. They should have been ongoing, as should have preventive measures to keep these survey measures well above unacceptable levels.

What kind of preventive measures? In the midst of change, it is too easy to attend to and reward those employees who are making the change happen. At rapidly changing firms like Cisco, poor souls such as Joan, who, in the midst of change chaos, tirelessly kept the firm's routine operations running and went the extra mile to serve existing customers, tend to be forgotten. Everyone else's attention is riveted on the internal challenge of pulling off the change and on the glory and rewards that come from leading the charge. Clearly such incentives are necessary in order to drive change. However, they need to be counter-balanced with incentives and rewards for those who are maintaining the stable operations that ultimately fund the current change as well as future ones. This is asking a lot of managers already involved in the turmoil of change, but one must consider the alternative.

Pacing During Industry Acceleration and Deceleration

Decelerating industries are industries in which the rate of environmentally imposed change is declining, or decelerating, and sta-bilization opportunities are increasing. Accelerating industries are the reverse. It is useful to discuss both together because they present virtu-ally opposite challenges and because resources freed up by industry deceleration need to be redeployed and recombined as soon as the industry begins to accelerate.

To continue with the example of Marburg Grace, currently, rapid changes caused by merger pressures have begun to subside. What should the company do now? Lick the wounds of a triple merger and move on? Alternatively, can it learn from its lessons and capitalize on what it learned during this period of brutal environmental turbulence and organizational change?

What to Do When the Industry Decelerates

Executives who are able to sense the onset of deceleration can antici-pate the threats it presents and start capitalizing on the opportunities it offers. What threats and what opportunities?

There are at least two key threats during deceleration. The first threat is that in the process of slowing down, the organization will stall and cramp up. What would be more natural after a period of extreme change such as Marburg Grace underwent than to stop changing entirely? What a mistake, however, if the firm goes from being change-aholic to being change averse. Deceleration, therefore, makes it necessary after a period to begin tracking not only the decline of initiative overload, which it should allow, but also the early signs of increasing organizational inertia. In these deceleration periods, companies have to begin implementing the tools that will be used more fully during periods of industry stability: fighting inertia, building change capacity, and stabilizing environments. A second threat to companies during a slowdown is allowing freed change resources to be absorbed into organizational fat and wasted on nonessential activities (e.g., all forms of corporate boondoggles and excesses) rather than using and retaining these resources efficiently.

The key opportunity during deceleration is to use these resources. This is one way to counter the growing inertia during deceleration regimes and the storing of released organizational resources into organizational fat rather than muscle. It is necessary to begin by cleaning up the messes left by the period of turbulence. Cisco has an urgent need to soothe its dissatisfied employees and customers, particularly those like Joan who already have one foot out the door.

What about when the change mess has been cleaned up? What comes next? The answer is straightforward: preparing the firm for the next acceleration regime.

Marburg Grace did not find the consultants that helped it manage its three mergers and postmerger integration processes very useful—in fact, the firm fired them. It decided instead to recombine the internal expertise it had developed through trial and error during the first two mergers, and which it recombined with great success during the third merger. To do so, it took a core staff of people who had played an important role in the three mergers and had them formalize and institutionalize the transition management structure that they had put in place to ease this third merger. This transition management structure had a merger management leader and a skilled merger management team with experience in managing three previous mergers, in monitoring their progress, and in taking corrective action before merger chaos reached impossible proportions. The informal network links that the team had built into various functions (e.g., legal and financial) were also formalized. Finally, measurement systems were formalized to make this transition structure increasingly cost effective. Indeed, the merger management team analyzed the three previous mergers not just with respect to change management procedures, but also with respect to the financial and human cost to the firm of these changes. During the next merger, not only would these costs be tracked in real time, but clear targets could be set concerning how much cheaper the change management cost of this merger would be compared with those in each of the previous three mergers.

What to Do When the Industry Accelerates

The challenges for an organization going through an acceleration regime parallel those of deceleration. Whereas the threat of deceleration was slowing the organizational change machinery without having it seize up, the threat that Marburg Grace will face when it moves into the next acceleration regime will be to warm up its change machinery without blowing all the gaskets. Doing so requires a new type of vigilance: not only actively tracking and attacking organizational inertia, but also becoming increasingly vigilant to indicators of initiative overload. Organizations may also find it necessary to create a few large, quick, visible, and successful changes in order to symbolize and communicate to employees that the organization is entering an acceleration phase.

Acceleration also means not eroding those change capacities that might become essential if a turbulent regime materializes and persists. Thus, companies should use some of the recombination change techniques discussed in this and previous chapters. They should then turn to more painful and destabilizing change techniques only as they become absolutely necessary.

Another challenge of acceleration is also the reverse of deceleration's challenge. During periods of excessive change, the organization is both running routine operations and managing change. Deceleration releases often substantial resources that were devoted to these change management tasks. During acceleration regimes, the opposite happens: The firm goes from running relatively routine operations to both running these operations and managing change. More resources have to be reassigned to change activities and to ramp-up activities.

Pacing During Placid Times in Your Industry

Firms can use three types of techniques for pacing during placid periods in the history of an industry, that is, periods during which externally imposed changes have slowed down drastically. One is to fight creeping inertia. The second is to build the firm's capacity to change and ready it for the next environmentally imposed acceleration regime. The third we already discussed in the section on turbulent regimes under the heading "Tools for Stabilizing Environments." The trick is to use these environmental stabilizing tools to delay, minimize, or block entirely the onset of acceleration regimes. Since this technique was already discussed, I turn to the other two respectively.

Fighting Inertia

It is placid regimes that remind us that pacing is not only about avoiding excessive change. It is also about avoiding excessive stability leading to inertia. Prolonged stability requires activities to retain the capacity to change when change becomes necessary.

During stable regimes, initiative overload vanishes. Rather, carefully scanning the company for indicators of mounting organizational inertia—and fighting it—becomes paramount. Crises, for instance, put a company on edge and counter inertia. But there is no need to invent artificial crises—real crises will arise soon enough. Fighting inertia, rather, involves surfacing potential threats, playing out crisis scenarios, and generally maintaining the company's change readiness.

Microsoft provides a good model for fighting inertia. Even during a period of its quasi-monopolistic dominance of competitors, Bill Gates was raising the specter of the next digital transformation that could bankrupt Microsoft. If you do not believe me, then read his book *The Road Ahead,* written at a point when Microsoft could not have been more dominant. Any Microsoft employee reading the book would have to have been convinced that Microsoft was on the verge of a precipice unless it prepared itself aggressively for the changes ahead.

Put differently, one challenge during placid regimes is keeping the company limber. This can be achieved by periodically getting the firm climbing the learning curve through a series of small, nondisruptive incremental changes. It may also be necessary to trigger a few larger and faster changes as well. This does not mean inventing a crisis, but rather capitalizing on opportunities for short sprints that keep the organization limber.

The best example may be the U.S. military, post-Vietnam. It wages an ongoing war against inertia by using simulated conflicts and war games against all forms of virtual enemies and competitors. At a minimum, managing during a placid, stable period requires a type of organizational gymnastics to keep organizations fit for change. This could mean small recombinatory changes with the five organizational elements found in your own corporate basement and discussed in chapters 3 through 7—in other words, reusing, redeploying, and recombining your people, networks, culture, processes, and structure to craft change with lesser pain.

Building Change Capacity

Does a firm's capacity to change remain fixed over time? In truth, no one has carried out research answering this question. Certain change theories assert that relentless change teaches firms to change more efficiently and helps their change capacity to increase over time, creating a virtuous cycle.

In my experience, however, this argument is valid only when the change load remains below change capacity. When it exceeds capacity frequently and consistently, it triggers not only repetitive-change syndrome, but also a vicious cycle by which this excessive change causes the change capacity to actually decline and further reinforces the depressing effects of repetitive-change syndrome.

Again, the example of Saul Steinberg at Steinberg, Inc., illustrates how a well-managed period of stability may allow a company's change capacity to build or rebuild. As one executive pointed out to me, his unit could run four-minute miles, so to speak, because it used the equivalent of athletic interval training rather than continuous training. Whereas continuous training means working out at the same pace over time, interval training involves fixed intervals of extreme activity that raise cardiovascular, muscular, and aerobic functions above normal levels, followed by recovery periods that bring all functions down below these levels. To avoid excessive pain and injury, the duration of recovery is gradually decreased, and exertion during activity phases is gradually increased, in order to continue raising the bar in athletic performance. Organizational interval training involves similar periods of extremely rapid change followed by periods of restorative stability, with the intent of raising firms' change capacity safely and effectively over time.

Much of the theorizing and advice on change management today calls for relentless change. As this chapter indicates, the alternative to the relentless-change approach is not so simple. Clearly the answer in rapidly changing environments cannot be to grind the wheel of change to a halt. It is too easy at this point to dust off another fable: "Be a turtle, not a hare. Move slowly and cautiously, and you will always get there faster." In truth, however, slowing down indiscriminately could provide the opportunity for competitors to speed past you.

Stability Without Pain

Change without pain at its core requires balancing stability with change in order to exploit the benefits of both and avoid the harm caused by either in isolation. Chapters 3 through 8 examined how using creative recombination, rather than creative destruction, would result in less pain in the midst of change. This chapter examined pacing, or when to alternate change (whether carried out by creative destruction or creative recombination) with periods of greater stability (that is, periods characterized by little or no change).

Clearly, as noted throughout this chapter, the pace at which both organizational change and the alternation between stability and change are carried out is never fully at the discretion of executives. The Web site ChangeWithoutPain.com directs the reader to ways of measuring environmental change, organizational change, and your firm's capacity to change. The judicious use of such measures reveals when and how quickly a firm must and can change. It also can determine when, how completely, and for how long a firm should attempt to avoid changing.

Moreover, the question addressed in this chapter has not been just when and how to change and to stabilize. The question has been, How can alternating stability and change actually make it easier to excel at both change management and at stability management? The formula, in a nutshell, is to fight organizational inertia during deceleration and placid regimes by making the changes necessary to help the firm fight excessive change during acceleration and turbulent regimes.

The next chapter concludes this book with an illustration of a design firm, IDEO, that exemplifies all of the principles and lessons of how an organization achieves change without pain. What makes such companies consistently able to accomplish so much recombinatory, innovative change? They rely on certain operating guidelines, which we will examine next.

10 Becoming a Better Recombiner

WALK INTO *IDEO, the design firm head-quartered in Palo Alto, California (with branch offices in Boston, Chicago, Grand Rapids, London, San Francisco, New York City, and Tokyo), and you will stumble onto what appears to be a gigantic mess. The office has an open, rambling architecture, bicycles and even an airplane wing hang from the ceiling, and a variety of books and magazines on wide-ranging topics line the tables and shelves. In fact, the company itself is an amalgam of disparate kinds of knowledge, individuals, tools, skill sets, machines, information, and styles. Product development meetings alternate between periods of disorganized chaos run by the "kids"— with their messes of spaghetti diagrams of linked ideas, techniques, and concepts crisscrossing the white boards—and periods of highly directed activity when there is a takeover by the "adults," the closest thing one will find to a manager at IDEO.*

Yet there is a kind of organization to this chaos, a capacity in the firm to hold onto this variety of human, technical, knowledge, and skill assets so pregnant with recombinatory possibilities—even though a particular end use might not be immediately evident. These elements do not even fit neatly into a categorization scheme that would make them easy to label and retrieve (in fact, such categorization would limit the creative thinking on which IDEO thrives), but within this mess, IDEO has a capacity to find the elements it needs to craft its innovations. Within the firm—the whole of which could be considered one enormous corporate basement—there are processes for finding and recombining elements (of what, to outsiders, looks like chaos) quickly and efficiently in highly ingenious solutions.

What's more, IDEO knows how to look outside the organization to find elements in the environment, in other organizations, and even in competitors' companies that it can recombine as well. Like a jazz musician, the company uses a wide range of "found objects" to improvise, reusing and recombining them apparently effortlessly and spontaneously to bring about successful transformations.

IDEO is a perfect example of many of the lessons and principles that I have been writing about throughout this book. More than just a cool, throw-me-the-Nerfball-dude type of company, it is a supremely efficient and highly profitable enterprise in which change and stability, flexibility and efficiency alternate in a stable balance. The result? IDEO has recombined its way to creating more than 4,000 successful products— including the Crest Neat Squeeze toothpaste tube, the 3Com Palm V, Apple Computer's PCMCIA card ejection system, the Steelcase Leap Chair, and second-generation balloon angioplasty devices, to name just a few.

What makes companies like IDEO able to consistently accomplish so much recombinatory, innovative change? Like many managerial practices, creative recombination is really as much an art as a science.

Nevertheless, according to my and others' research, organizations that recombine most successfully rely on certain operating guidelines that would assist most any company in crafting effective, cost-efficient change without pain. Let us look at each principle in turn.

Tip 1: Give Serious Consideration to Children's Velcro Suits and Surgical Weed Whackers

Consider an IDEO brainstorming session. A group of engineers are arrayed around a table trying to develop better skin surgery techniques. One engineer pipes up and proposes miniaturized "weed whackers" to trim skin tissue during surgery. No one at the table bats an eyelash. Now witness another recombination session—this one to invent a better shopping cart. The problem at hand: how to secure the children in the cart more safely. A different engineer proposes yet another "interesting" solution—put children in Velcro suits to attach them to the cart. No one even winces. To the uninitiated, this might seem like complete lunacy. But David Kelley, IDEO's CEO, makes the point that it is often the crazy ideas that provide the breakthrough that can be reused, redeployed, and recombined to come up with the ideal solution.

Kelley could not be more on point. Resist the temptation to apply twenty-twenty hindsight, and ask yourself, Is the child's Velcro suit or the surgical weed whacker any more bizarre than some of the masterful recombinations that we have seen throughout this book? Is it any stranger than Gutenberg making a printing press out of a wine press and a coin stamping machine? Or than Dow Corning turning an industrial coating into Saran Wrap? Or Sony recombining movie studios, consumer electronics, and broadband technology? Or GKN turning a practice of lending out engineers after contract cancellations into an engineer employment agency?

Not surprisingly, three of the five rules that govern recombining at IDEO have to do with tolerating deviant ideas: (1) encourage wild ideas, (2) defer judgment, and (3) build on the ideas of others. The other two rules are there to maintain some order and sanity during the recombination process: (4) one conversation at a time and (5) stay focused on the topic. The larger point here is that it is difficult to recombine if there is nothing interesting to recombine. Paradoxically, the ability to create new recombinants requires having the permission to take crazy risks and even fail in creating new recombinants. That doesn't mean taking uncontrolled risks or failing repeatedly in the same way. It doesn't mean failing when failure is preventable, or failing when even successes would be of little value. Rather, it means having permission to fail while taking the risk to recombine in an inspired fashion.

Indeed, nothing kills the impulse to add to the supply of a firm's recombinants than the type of punishment that is dished out in so many organizations for failed recombiners. I remember one such "failure"—a rising star whose career had exploded with the dot-com bubble. His only crime had been to attempt to recombine the firm's existing operation with a Web interface. As e-commerce became unfashionable, FAILURE was branded on his forehead, a sign well known in this firm to mean that your career there would never go anywhere.

Consider also an example I mentioned in a previous chapter. I was working with a team at Marburg Grace, a European financial services firm, exploring how to recombine successful IT resources across the firm. What I did not mention is that three days into the job, we found out by chance that a prior attempt to recombine IT had not succeeded. Why did it not succeed? No one could tell us. "Why can't we find out this type of information?" I asked. Because, I was told, at Marburg Grace, divulging information about a failure meant that you were involved in that failure, and failure involvement is career limiting. So whereas success has many, many parents, at Marburg Grace, failure is an orphan. At IDEO, by contrast, the children's Velcro suit and the surgical weed whacker are experiments that are not just allowed to be voiced, but are encouraged—and for which no one is punished, but rather for which people are rewarded.

Tip 2: Encourage Messes, Messiness, and Messing Up

One Columbia University professor tells the story of how and where he came up with his Nobel Prize–winning bolt of insight. Where? Atop his incredibly messy desk, covered by layers upon layers of articles. How? By the chance juxtaposition of two apparently unrelated articles in the massive clutter on his desk, and by the insight this

created: The two ideas in the "unrelated" articles were in fact inti-
mately related and provided the solution to a problem that had vexed
his field of biology for decades.

Consider now this description of an IDEO engineer's office from a
team of scholars who studied IDEO in depth. The office "had a
chrome-plated plastic nameplate from an Isuzu Trooper, a 1950s
Hamilton Beach blender, molded rubber ears from a past project on
headsets, the final headset and several early prototypes, toy cars that
contained flywheels, a butane torch that runs on a cigarette lighter, an
oversized computer trackball for kids, the prototype for that product
made of machined aluminum and electrical components, several surgical products he had designed, and a toy dartgun."[1] This mess of objects
was often used by the engineers as elements that could be drawn from
and recombined in new ways to come up with novel recombinations.

Once again, the larger point is that keeping recombinants in a
tight, neat little ordering scheme makes them easy to find. But this ease
of retrieval comes at a cost. The recombinants are never put "out of
order" in a way that suggests how they might be recombined into a
new order. If you keep your work tools in one area and your kitchen
appliances in another, you will tend to overlook how the potato
masher might serve as a very good hammer that does not dent the two
dovetailed pieces of wood that you are trying to pound together. If you
walk through IDEO, you will not find a neat ordering of offices, where
different types of specialists are separated in different areas and on different floors. Rather, there is a mess of offices and cubicles that puts
people with completely different knowledge and skills in close proxim-
ity so that they may learn from each other and find lucky recombinations of their varied expertise.

Tip 3: Hire Jills of a Few Trades and Apprentices of Most

It is simple enough to think of the recombinant properties of
electrical components. Devices with a common standard—electrical
plugs and sockets, for instance—are recombinable. But what defines the
recombinant properties of an individual? Clearly, not the narrow over-
specialization that renders individuals compatible only with similar
narrow specialists. What is needed is not cogs capable of interacting

only with other like cogs, but rather people with diverse characteristics who are recombinable with one another—be it their knowledge, skills, aptitudes, cognitive styles, or values.

This does not mean that such recombinable people are Jacks of all trades and masters of none. Rather, they are a particular type of generalist—what might be called Jills of a few trades. That is, people who can develop mastery in two or three areas of expertise and have a core understanding of many. Jills of a few trades have multiple facets to their skills, backgrounds, and personalities that render them compatible with many other types of people because they share not only diverse skills that allow them to complement each other, but also some similar characteristics that allow them to bond.

IDEO is a company that has many Jills, who can be decombined from teams and recombined into new teams capable of designing modules and bundles as diverse as the 3Com Palm V or the Crest Neat Squeeze toothpaste tube. Whenever a design team is needed, the facilitator (as IDEO calls the team head) invites people with the right mix of different and complementary skills necessary for the job at hand.

So how do you know who are your Jills of a few trades? They are often boundary spanners. They don't eat lunch with the same coworkers every day. Their friends are not clones of each other, sharing the same perspectives on life. They have friends who are rock musicians, plumbers, nuclear physicists. They travel a lot—and not in tour buses. They like to try different things and are easily bored. Jills have a broad array of ideas and techniques, and as a result they have at their fingertips the raw materials for recombination. At IDEO, for instance, it is considered particularly cool during a design meeting to bring in ideas from hobbies such as remote control airplanes or sailing.

Not everyone in a firm needs to be a Jill of a few trades, however. Jills serve as interfaces that help combine otherwise incompatible people. They are people with big, wide-ranging networks—what I called network hubs in chapters 3 and 4—who can connect with people who have much smaller, narrow, and specialized networks. They are the equivalent of the converter plug that allows me to plug my German, U.S.-compatible razor into an Italian power socket. M.B.A.'s trained as generalists, with one or more specializations, can often serve this function, as can individuals who have worked cross functionally or across different firms or parts of their firm.

Tip 4: Encourage a Culture of Homogeneous Diversity

Many popular management books will tell you that a strong homogeneous culture is important for a firm to exploit synergies between its parts. These books by homogenists can be hard to reconcile with another type of popular management book by heterogenists, who advocate the precise opposite—cultures of diversity in firms. These popular books urge us to value heterogeneous cultures for the diversity of perspectives they bring. Many executives have trouble reconciling these cultural diversity and homogeneity imperatives, just as most people find it hard to reconcile the cliché "birds of a feather flock together" with another cliché, "opposites attract." The problem, of course, is that both homogenists and heterogenists overgeneralize and overstate their claims, with the result that the delicate balance between cultural homogeneity and diversity necessary to sustain recombination and painless change is obscured.

Organizational cultures are a double-edged sword when it comes to recombination and pacing. On the plus side, a successful element developed in one part of a strong homogenous culture will more likely be compatible and recombinable with another element developed in another part of the culture—just as two people from Germany meeting in New York City for the first time are likely to get along better than if one of them was from a non-German-speaking part of Italy. Strong, homogeneous cultures heighten the likelihood that organizational successes can and will be reused, redeployed, and recombined across different parts of a firm. Indeed, strong homogeneous cultures turn individuals acting at cross purposes into one organization acting with a common purpose. They allow everybody to read off the same page and to fire from the same side of the ship.

The disadvantage of strong cultures, however, is that everybody is reading from the same page and firing on the same spot. Put differently, in strong cultures, like in cults, everybody thinks and behaves alike, and an important element of diversity is lost. Change without pain requires not just the act of recombination, but also a variety of elements that can be recombined. If everyone thinks and behaves the same, then it is also likely that they will not produce the diversity of elements necessary to recombine effectively.

For an organization to have the capacity to recombine itself, it has to be made of subcultures bound together by a common culture. That is, it must balance within itself the opposite poles of strong homogeneity and diversity. The cultural diversity encourages the creation of the varied elements to be combined, whereas the homogeneity makes the combinations possible.

Tip 5: Reward Those Who Give and Use Junk

Guidelines such as encouraging crazy ideas, tolerating messes, hiring Jills of a few trades, or valuing balanced cultural homogeneity and diversity might leave you with the impression that the only advice for pacing and recombining is to generate a wide variety of recombinants. Nothing could be further from the truth. Firms that are expert only at generating recombinants can easily end up generating a lot of what the Nobel laureate Sydney Brenner calls "garbage"—the stuff that can never be recombined. What is needed is not garbage, but rather what he calls "junk"—the stuff that you keep around the basement workshop and which can become useful in a pinch. If IDEO ever stops producing useful junk and recombining it, it will become an example of how not to recombine.

Indeed, it is not sufficient to have some good junky recombinants rather than a bunch of garbage. There must also exist very strict guidelines that encourage people to actually contribute new and better junk to the basement workshop and to get rid of old, soon-to-be-garbage junk that is cluttering everything up. Relatedly, people in firms must be able not only to *find* the good junky recombinants, but also must *find it in their interest* to look for such junk, to reuse it, and to recombine it. In a world in which work, change, and knowledge overload employees, managers, and leaders, it cannot be assumed that people will naturally go around looking for junky recombinants. Indeed, if time (to search for recombinants) is money, then people may be reluctant to discover that such searches are cost-effective until they are encouraged to do so. Finally, for people to find good junk, those who make it must also find it in their interest to take the time to circulate their junk.

Consider the problem of both circulating junk and of using junk that is being circulated. As I travel across organizations, I hear frequent complaints from people who developed magnificent recombinants that were then cloned widely throughout the firm without any rewards to their creators, let alone a thank you. Similarly, I hear complaints from people who recombined existing assets rather than paying for someone to reinvent them, yet who received no recognition or rewards for the cost savings to the firm. On the flip side, those who reinvented the wheel, sometimes repeatedly, suffered no consequences.

In short, in many firms, no good deed goes unpunished. The rewards go only to those who reach objectives, not to those who spend time providing and using the firm's recombinants. Paradoxically, then, the lack of incentives to recombine are in effect a reward to people throughout the firm for reinventing the wheel rather than recombining the wheels the firm already possesses.

But organizations that effect change without pain know better. In organizations that artfully recombine junk, there is no greater sin than to reinvent an existing recombinant. It is a reflex in these firms to examine what has already been done and what recombinants already exist before attempting any new activity. And they find that what gets measured gets done and what gets rewarded gets done repeatedly. In other words, the supply, processing, demand, and consumption of recombinants can be encouraged by leveraging existing measurement and reward processes.

One IDEO engineer, for instance, described rewards for "spreading your knowledge and your skills around because you get to be seen by more people and you become more desirable to work with." Indeed, at IDEO, your status as an engineer depends greatly on what junky recombinants you are contributing to others.

Other firms have more formal systems. At Booz•Allen & Hamilton, the consulting firm, what gets measured includes the number of Web site queries for a particular recombinant contributed by a consultant, and formal ratings assess how much he or she provided, as well as support know-why and know-how. At Columbia University, there are similar rewards for contributing and drawing upon recombinants. The use of one scholar's recombinant by another scholar has to be acknowledged in published articles using bibliographic reference to the other's work. Such referencing becomes an indicator of a scholar's contributions to a field's recombinant pool of research theories, findings, and research techniques. For example, I can pull up the Social Science Citation Index on the World Wide Web and find out how many times my work has been cited. I can then compare my contributions to the field with those of other scholars who have been cited more or less than I have. A scholar's stature and opportunity for promotion is established by peer ratings, by the number of articles she publishes, and by how frequently her work is cited. That is how an internal market for recombinants is created and encouraged at a university.

Tip 6: Beg, Borrow, Copy, and Celebrate

The motto of one firm I worked with recently was B2C2—beg, borrow, copy, and celebrate. This company valued shameless borrowing. Of course, by shameless, they did not mean slavish; there's little value in applying all ideas in a cookie-cutter fashion. This firm knew when it was time to clone, to customize, or to translate the best elements of an idea, process, structure, or product in order to recombine it. Moreover, this firm was not unique: The core values of the balanced firms that I have had the pleasure to watch have been a deep skepticism for invention alone and a strong penchant for a careful balance of invention and recombination.

The norm in B2C2 companies is a willingness to noodle with what already exists and to invent from scratch only later. Here too, we can take a number of lessons from IDEO. Consider an IDEO project manager describing the early stages of designing a new kitchen appliance: "The best way to come up with ideas was first of all to go out and look at what's out there. Look at the existing products, rip them apart, then look for peripheral objects, like toasters, blenders, and mixers. When you find technical problems, go out, look around, and walk around ripping apart possibly relevant products."[2] Moreover, B2C2 is better if it is wide ranging, looking everywhere to find the best ideas to steal ruthlessly. IDEO's CEO David Kelley makes this very clear: "Working with companies in such dissimilar industries as medical instruments, furniture, toys, and computers has given us a broad view of the latest technologies available and has taught us how to do quality product development and how to do it quickly and efficiently."[3]

It should be clear that in firms like IDEO, this B2C2 mentality is a priority. Indeed, as I mentioned earlier, what is the use of developing a wide range of recombinants if nobody uses them? Take the example of McKinsey, the consulting firm. One partner explains that every morning, it is normal to find on one's desk a number of queries about whether a McKinsey solution already exists to a particular client problem. He points out that it is normal for him to answer these requests first and then go on with his own work, rather than leaving them to the end of the day—if time permits. Likewise, it would be a clear violation of the company's norms to solve a client problem only to be shown that a McKinsey solution to that problem had already been developed.

Following such values and norms of shameless borrowing isn't easy. In cultures like that of the United States, imitation is seen as a sign of weakness, if not moral turpitude. Imitators are seen as people who aren't smart enough to invent good ideas for themselves. But words such as *copycat* and *impersonator* should be compliments, not insults. Companies need cultures that value creative imitation and condemn invention that is wasteful. An IDEO designer put it in these terms:

> What it really is, I mean, it's kind of a state of mind. Where I worked before, you just didn't ask for help. It was a sign of weakness. What they thought brainstorming was compared to what we think it is are very different things. We don't have time to screw around. At the first hint I don't know something, I'll ask "Does anyone know about this?" The whole thing here is you've got to leverage as much as possible. You ask for help. You are expected to ask for help here.[4]

Likewise, another IDEO employee who worked on an electric vehicle charging station for GM/Hughes indicated how he got "unstuck": "I couldn't make one part clear another part. I didn't know how to put a hinge on it. I called a 45-minute brainstorm with 5 people. Three minutes before the end, one of the designers, she came up with an idea that became the final design."[5]

Tip 7: Look Inside to Chief Memory Officers

You'll recall from chapter 2 the story of Westland Helicopters, which found itself in the post–Cold War era needing to become more competitive in its production of helicopters. Rather than bringing in a cadre of consultants or seeking other kinds of outside solutions, the executives found new ways of developing its product more cost-efficiently right there within its own division and at its parent company.

But recombining can also involve going outside the firm to find existing elements that can be recombined with existing internal elements. That isn't necessarily a bad thing, but it is a question of balance. The problem is that firms that value external recombinants over internal recombinants tend to look outside *first*—for hires, for merger partners, for consultants or for the latest hot idea—rather than looking first to internal promotions, organic growth, and their own employees' and executives' hot ideas. Such values and norms tend to focus firms on the riskiest forms of recombination. Firms that use external recombinants always run the risk of seeing these recombinants rejected because of what I call *tissue rejection*—the tendency of a firm to reject ideas, technologies, and practices from outside its boundaries. Recombining external elements therefore requires the use of techniques for fooling a firm's immune system. Relying more on internal recombinants does not.

Valuing *both* internal and external capacities, then—and not just external capacities—is important because it orients firms to start with less risky recombination and balance it with external parts when necessary. Likewise, it may be necessary to balance the use of not only *new* recombinants, but of *antiquated* ones as well. It should be normal to look back into a firm's history, learn its past successes, and revive them on the road to future successes. As a result, the inventory of recombinants grows from those that we have on hand to include those that we can actively remember.

That was the case in at least three examples that we looked at earlier in this book: Sony, Mercedes-Benz, and Apple Computer. You'll recall that in each of these companies, someone had the wisdom to delve into the company's past and revive an old value or product philosophy in order to craft a "new" way of solving a pressing business problem. Whether it be Werner Niefer at Mercedes, Steve Jobs at Apple Computer, or Nobuyuki Idei at Sony, these leaders serve a dual function. They not only provide charismatic leadership, they also serve as the organization's memory. Some companies hire historians to write their histories, whereas others remember the simple truth that their long-tenured employees are their best historians. These "chief memory officers" are informally asked to look back over past projects, successful and unsuccessful, before any "innovation" is launched or *relaunched*. Every company needs memory keepers with the clout to make themselves heard. They help the organization undertake change without engendering unnecessary chaos, cynicism, or burnout.

But the opposite is also true: Not all things that a company did in the past are wonderful and good. And as we all know, people who do not understand history are doomed to relive it. Valuing the past, therefore, also means looking back into the firm's history to see whether a proposed change was attempted previously and what its outcome was and why. Organizations that have such a norm in place are less likely to waste change resources by repeating the same mistakes again and again, or to ignore perfectly good solutions that did not work once because of past conditions but could be highly effective given current conditions.

Past-oriented values and norms also halt pendulum changes in firms like Exide (which I described in chapter 7) as well as the waste of change resources that happens in too many organizations. Values and norms that focus attention on a firm's past reveal the pendulum swings between trade-offs and focus the firm's attention on how to achieve a balance between these trade-offs. By reducing the waste of change resources and by allowing for balance, these values play an important role in pacing periods of stability and periods of change.

Tip 8: Have Standards

Consider the group of executives at the European financial services firm, Marburg Grace, who were befuddled by how difficult it was for their firm to recombine its information technology assets. With a little analysis, they realized that their firm's culture valued rapid service from the IT department, whether or not what was developed was compatible with other installed IT elements and could be reused. More concretely, it was normal for the IT department to program a piece of customer management software in two weeks, rather than taking a third week to give the software a standardized, clear interface that would render it easily recombinable with other software in and around the firm. In short, at least in the case of IT, this firm had no standards. More generally, it should come as no surprise to firms that have standards but do not enforce them that recombination will therefore require much more customization and translation than is absolutely necessary.

Not all recombinants are amenable to the type of standardization possible with IT recombinants. Nonetheless, some structural mechanism has to turn recombinants into information about the existence of these recombinants. IDEO archives the recombinants it develops in reports and in videotapes. Scholars studying IDEO, for example, "saw one designer ask another for a brainstorming report about flexible surgical tubing to get ideas about designing a personal appliance. Another designer said that he sometimes watches old videotapes of especially fruitful brainstorms so that he doesn't forget the 'cool' ideas he learned."[6]

Chapter 2 discussed the varying types of knowledge that have to accompany recombinants for them to be reused, redeployed, and recombined successfully: Know-what, know-why, know-who, and know-who-knows-who are essential for customizing and translating recombinants before they can be recombined. Standardizing such information and knowledge makes recombination all the easier. Firms that excel at recombining all insist that information and knowledge about recombinants be captured in a carefully scripted, defined, and standardized language. These languages can become rich with clearly defined terms of art—the very terms that appear as daunting jargon to outsiders and non-cognoscenti. Indeed, know-what, know-why and know-who must be clear in this standardized language so as to make recombinants available in an unambiguous fashion to other members of these organizations.

At Booz•Allen, for instance, this linguistic standardization is accomplished by teams of editors who homogenize the language by which recombinants are communicated to the rest of the firm. They are also responsible for keeping the information and knowledge about recombinants current, adding new ones periodically and discarding the obsolete. This avoids recombining inferior recombinants or recombinants that had been shown to fail previously when better ones have already been created.

Indeed, "garbage in, garbage out," the saying goes. A firm that disseminates and recombines inferior ideas, processes, values, products, and human capital will produce inferior recombinants. If the supply of successful recombinants is important, then their screening for quality is paramount. Organizations forget, as they upload information about recombinants onto elaborate Web sites, that there must be continuous sifting, inclusion into, and rejection from a firm's inventory of recombinants as new recombinants materialize and as old ones become obsolete or are proven ineffective. Put differently, the recombinant pool requires careful upkeep and updating.

It may come as a surprise that the organizing processes of schools and universities—dedicated to the creation and dissemination of innovative knowledge—are very suspicious of innovations. Or rather, quality control is paramount. Each cold-fusion claim is subjected to extreme scrutiny, and innovators have to make a strong case that they have developed something new and true that should be added to the corpus of recombinable knowledge in the field. The onus is on them to prove that they are not the authors of just another crack-pot idea, of old wine in new bottles, or of the next fad. Careful review of what has already been done in a field is the norm, as is extremely careful empirical testing of innovative knowledge claims.

Indeed, most top-rated academic journals accept less than 10 percent of the articles that are submitted. This means that 90 percent of claims to new knowledge are rejected. A process of anonymous reviewing guarantees that contributions are judged on their merit rather than on the political power of the contributor. Moreover, scholars are penalized by their academic institutions for publishing too many articles in low-quality journals. Promotions are based on elaborate processes for judging the quality of scholars' output. At Columbia Business School, no fewer than thirty specialists in the field can be asked to comment on whether a professor should be promoted, and less than nearly unanimous and enthusiastic support blocks promotion.

Tip 9: Our Employees Are Our Most Precious Asset

Just because something is a worn cliché does not mean that it is wrong or that it cannot take on new and exciting meaning. Such is the case with the adage that to succeed, firms must value their people above almost everything else.

Yet, almost every guru of change management will at one point or another present the metaphor of the burning platform of change. It sits there, aflame, perched on one side of the canyon. As employees begin to smolder, they find in themselves a sudden motivation to overcome their purportedly innate resistance to change and to hurl themselves toward the relative comfort of the canyon's other wall. If, in that change process, they get slightly toasted—well, no pain no change, right? Besides, a little change management burn ointment can always be applied to grease the process. Moreover, as people fling themselves burning through the air, these change gurus assure us, the promised vision of a pleasant, cool, comfortable platform sitting on the other canyon edge comes into view. Employees will quickly forget the discomfort of their second-degree burns and rejoice in their newfound workplace. Presumably, this new platform is itself kerosene soaked, in preparation for the next revolutionary canyon leap.

Good creative recombiners, on the other hand, hold values and follow norms of behavior that attempt to spare employees change-related pain. They recognize that sometimes "no pain equals no change" is true—but that it is also true that sometimes "all pain equals no change." They ardently believe that less pain could result in more change.

The Low Road to Change

In conclusion, the masters of change that I have had the privilege to know did not change for change's sake. They kept things stable when stability was right, and they made changes only when they were necessary. Rather than taking the high road to change, they were recombiners. They did not climb the mountain in search of a far-reaching vision. They did not have big audacious goals. They did not stare for long hours at a blank sheet of paper in search of the next winning corporate innovation. They did not produce strategies and businesses of exquisite beauty and originality in order to obliterate the ugly remnants of the past.

Rather than going to the top of the mountain, they went to the corporate basement, so to speak. They gathered discarded organizational parts that were lying around. They pulled them together rapidly into ugly but highly ingenious solutions to their problems. They did not invent, nor did they want to. They cut corners, borrowed shamelessly, took short cuts, imitated, and settled for second-hand, inferior components to build solutions. They slapped together hopeful monsters that scared people or made them laugh. The founder of FedEx, you'll recall, got a C in his business school entrepreneurship class for proposing an absurd recombination of second-hand airplanes and trucks, credit cards, bar code technology, wheel-and-spoke route structures, and mailing envelopes that became one of the most successful express mail carriers in history.

In the end, these recombiners have changed the world more rapidly, smoothly, cheaply, and successfully than anyone who traveled the high road to change.

Notes

Introduction

1. Ronald G. Verona, "Education for your Life," <http://www.education 4yourlife.org/> (accessed 8 April 2003).

2. Richard Foster and Sarah Kaplan, *Creative Destruction: Why Companies That Are Built to Last Underperform the Market, and How to Successfully Transform Them* (New York: Doubleday/Currency 2001).

3. See in particular, Eric Abrahamson, "Management Fashion," *Academy of Management Review* 21 (1986): 254–285; Eric Abrahamson and Gregory Fairchild, "Management Fashion: Life Cycle, Triggers, and Collective Learning Processes," *Administrative Science Quarterly* 4 (1999): 708–740; and Eric Abrahamson, "Fads and Fashions in Administrative Technologies" (Ph.D. diss., New York University, 1989).

4. Useful books are John Mickletwait and Adrian Wooldridge, *The Witch Doctors* (London: Heinemann, 1997); Andrzej A. Huczynski, *Popular Management Ideas* (London: Routledge, 1993); José Luis Alvarez, ed., *The Diffusion and Consumption of Business Knowledge* (London: MacMillan Press, 1998); and Brad Jackson, *Management Gurus and Management Fashions* (London: Routledge, 2001).

5. See, in particular, Françoise Chevalier, *Cercles de qualité et changement organizationnel* (Paris: Economica, 1993); and Mark J. Zbaracki, "The Rhetoric and Reality of Total Quality Management," *Administrative Science Quarterly* 42, no. 3 (1998): 602–636.

6. Eric Abrahamson and Micki Eisenman, "Why Management Scholars Must Intervene Strategically in the Management Knowledge Market," *Human Relations* 54, no. 1 (2001): 67–76.

7. Abrahamson and Fairchild, "Management Fashion."

Chapter 1

1. Richard Foster and Sarah Kaplan, *Creative Destruction: Why Companies That Are Built to Last Underperform the Market, and How to Successfully Transform Them* (New York: Doubleday/Currency, 2001).

2. For a comprehensive review of the scientific research in this area, go to <http://www.ChangeWithoutPain.com>.

3. See, for instance, William P. Barnett and John Freeman, "Too Much of a Good Thing? Product Proliferation and Organizational Failure," *Organizational Science* 12, no. 5 (2001): 539–558.

4. David Halberstam, *The Reckoning* (New York: Morrow/Avon, 1986).

5. Paul Lawrence and Davis Dyer, *Renewing American Industry: Organizing for Efficiency and Innovation* (New York: Free Press, 1983).

6. See, for instance, Lynne M. Andersson, "Employee Cynicism: An Examination Using a Contract Violation Framework," *Human Relations* 49 (1996): 1395–1418; James W. Dean Jr., Pamela Brandes, and Ravi Dharwadkar, "Organizational Cynicism," *Academy of Management Review* 23 (1998): 341–352; Sep Chichester, Lynne M. Andersson, and Thomas S. Bateman, "Cynicism in the Workplace: Some Causes and Effects," *Journal of Organizational Behavior* 18 (1998): 449–469; and John P. Wanous et al., "Cynicism About Organizational Change," *Group and Organization Management* 25, no. 2 (2000): 132–154.

7. Arnon E. Reichers, John P. Wanous, and James T. Austin, "Understanding and Managing Cynicism About Organizational Change," *Academy of Management Executive* 11, no. 1 (1998): 48–59.

8. Wilmar Schaufeli and Dirk Enzmann, *The Burnout Companion to Study and Practice: A Critical Analysis* (London: Taylor and Francis, 1998).

9. Wikipedia: The Free Encyclopedia, <http://www.wikipedia.org> (accessed 4 April, 2002).

10. Tom Clausen, Lecture at Columbia University, New York.

11. Jay W. Lorsch, Cyrus F. Gibson, and John A. Seeger, "First National Citibank Operating Group (A) and (B)," Teaching Note 493-024 (Boston, Harvard Business School, 1992).

12. Darrell K. Rigby, *Management Tools Global Results: Annual Survey of Senior Executives* (Boston: Bain & Company, 2002).

13. Kurt Lewin, *Field Theory in Social Science* (New York: Harper and Rowe, 1951).

Chapter 3

1. Kim S. Cameron, "Strategic Organizational Downsizing: An Extreme Case," *Research in Organizational Behavior* 20 (1998): 185–229.

2. Edward C. Murphy, *Strategies for Health Care Excellence* (Washington, DC: American Society for Work Redesign, 1994).

3. Todd D. Jick and Mary Gentile, "Peter Browning and Continental White Cap (A), (B), (C)," Teaching Note 5-491-110 (Boston: Harvard Business School, 2000).

4. Donald C. Hambrick, "The Top Management Team: Key to Strategic Success," *California Management Review* 30 (1987): 88–109.

5. Todd D. Jick and Mary Gentile, "Peter Browning and Continental White Cap," video, product number 9-887-502 (Boston: Harvard Business School Publishing, 1986).

6. U.S. Department of Commerce, Economics and Statistics Administration and Bureau of the Census, *Population Projections of the United States by Age, Sex, Race, and Hispanic Origin: 1995 to 2050* (Washington, DC: U.S. Census Bureau, 1999).

7. Joan Raymond, "The Jaws of Victory," *Newsweek,* 18 March 2002, 38.

Chapter 4

1. Russell A. Eisenstat, "Managing Xerox's Multinational Development Center," Teaching Note 9-490-029 (Boston: Harvard Business School, 1989).

2. M. Diane Burton, Hannah Riley, and Stephanie Woerner, "Jerry Sanders," Teaching Note 5-400-008 (Boston, Harvard Business School, 2000).

3. Wayne Baker, *Achieving Success Through Social Capital* (San Francisco: Jossey-Bass, 2000).

4. Nan Lin, Ronald S. Burt, and Karen S. Cook, eds., *Social Capital: Theory and Research* (New York: Aldine de Gruyter, 2001).

5. David Stamps, "Off the Charts," *Training* 34, no. 10 (1997): 77–84.

Chapter 6

1. Darrell K. Rigby, *Management Tools Global Results: Annual Survey of Senior Executives* (Boston: Bain & Company, 2002).

2. Ibid.

3. David Knights and Hugh Willmott, eds., *The Re-engineering Revolution: Critical Studies of Corporate Change* (London: Sage, 2000).

4. Michael Polanyi, *Personal Knowledge: Towards a Post-Critical Philosophy* (Chicago: University of Chicago Press, 1974).

5. Frederic M. Scherer, "Inter-industry Technology Flows in the United States," *Research Policy* 11 (1982): 227–245.

Chapter 7

1. Joann S. Lublin, "Division Problem—Place vs. Product: It's Tough to Choose a Management Model—Exide Tore Up System Based on Countries for One Centered on Battery Lines—Rolling Over European Fiefs," *The Wall Street Journal,* 27 June 2001, A1.

2. Michael Beer, Michael Tushman, and John J. Gabarro, "SMA: Micro-Electronic Products Division (A)," Case 9-400-084 (Boston: Harvard Business School, 2000).

3. Richard S. Dunham, "Q&A: Nokia's Ollila on CEO Profiles and the Company's Future," *Business Week,* 10 August 1988.

4. Françoise Chevalier, *Cercles de qualité et changement organizationnel* (Paris: Economica, 1993).

Chapter 8

1. Herminia Ibarra and Gillian Morris, "Ethan Berman at RiskMetrics Group (A) and (B)," Teaching Note 5-401-016 (Boston: Harvard Business School, 2000).

2. Ibid.

3. Pankaj Ghemawat and Bret Baird, "Leadership Online: Barnes & Noble vs. Amazon.com (A)," Case 9-798-063 (Boston: Harvard Business School, 1998).

4. Ibid.

Chapter 9

1. Roger Hallowell, "Sears, Roebuck and Co. (A): Turnaround," Case 9-898-007 (Boston: Harvard Business School, 1997).

2. Henry Mintzberg and James A. Watter, "Tracking Strategy in an Entrepreneurial Firm," *Academy of Management Journal* 25 (1982): 465–499.

3. Linda Argote and Dennis Epple, "Learning Curves in Manufacturing," *Science* 247 (1990): 920–924.

4. Peter Brabeck and Suzy Wetlaufer, "The Business Case Against Revolution: An Interview with Nestlé's Peter Brabeck," *Harvard Business Review,* February 2001.

5. Ibid.

Chapter 10

1. Robert I. Sutton and Andrew Hargadon, "Brainstorming Groups in Context: Effectiveness in a Product Design Firm," *Administrative Science Quarterly* 41 (1996): 685–718.

2. Andrew B. Hargadon, "Firms as Knowledge Brokers: Lessons in Pursuing Continuous Innovation," *California Management Review* 40 (1998): 209–227.

3. Ibid.

4. Sutton and Hargadon, "Brainstorming Groups in Context."

5. Ibid.

6. Ibid.

Index

About the Author

Eric Abrahamson is a tenured full professor of management at Columbia Business School. He holds degrees from New York University (Ph.D. and M.Ph.). After teaching at New York University, Professor Abrahamson joined the Columbia Business School faculty in 1989. He was a visiting professor at INSEAD, France, in 1999.

Professor Abrahamson is an active consultant and instructor in corporate executive education programs around the world. He is internationally recognized for his research on innovative techniques for managing organizations and their employees. His work has won two of the most prestigious awards in the management area, the award for the best article published in the *Academy of Management Journal* (1995) and two best paper awards of the Academy of Management Organization and Management Theory Division (1990, 1997). He is a past consulting editor for the *Academy of Management Review* and chair of the Organization and Management Theory Division of the Academy of Management. He has published numerous articles and book chapters that have appeared in the *Administrative Science Quarterly,* the *Academy of Management Journal,* the *Academy of Management Review, Computational and Mathematical Organizational Theory,* the *Journal of Management Studies, Harvard Business Review, Human Relations,* the *Journal of Organizational Behavior, Organization Science, Research in Organizational Behavior,* and the *Journal of Business Finance and Accounting.*